THE SPACE OF MIRACLES

A Journey With a Gypsy Samurai

GEORGE J. TANI, DDIV., MBA, LCSW-R

BALBOA.PRESS
A DIVISION OF HAY HOUSE

Balboa Press books may be ordered through booksellers or by contacting:

Balboa Press
A Division of Hay House
1663 Liberty Drive
Bloomington, IN 47403
www.balboapress.com
844-682-1282

Because of the dynamic nature of the Internet, any web addresses or
links contained in this book may have changed since publication and
may no longer be valid. The views expressed in this work are solely those
of the author and do not necessarily reflect the views of the publisher,
and the publisher hereby disclaims any responsibility for them.

The author of this book does not dispense medical advice or prescribe the use
of any technique as a form of treatment for physical, emotional, or medical
problems without the advice of a physician, either directly or indirectly. The
intent of the author is only to offer information of a general nature to help
you in your quest for emotional and spiritual well-being. In the event you use
any of the information in this book for yourself, which is your constitutional
right, the author and the publisher assume no responsibility for your actions.

Any people depicted in stock imagery provided by Getty Images are
models, and such images are being used for illustrative purposes only.
Certain stock imagery © Getty Images.

Print information available on the last page.

ISBN: 978-1-9822-7838-0 (sc)
ISBN: 978-1-9822-7839-7 (e)

Balboa Press rev. date: 12/09/2021

Contents

Acknowledgement

My wife Rosalyn Tani has been a steadfast contributor to the development of this book. She has contributed insights as well as interpersonal dynamics clarifying the essence of many experiences. She as well provided continued associations, connections, and meanings to outcomes. Gene Maniscalco in the initial stages of formulating the book was an important contributor in reviewing the formatting of many of the experiences of my book adding clarity and meaning to various chapters in the book. Many good wishes to my dear friend, colleague, and mentor, Dr. Justine Pawlukewicz. She has provided me with guidance and friendship in this journey of sharing my own with others.

This book is dedicated to

God Supreme Intervention in the life of human kind.

Introduction

What forces of nature, history, serendipity, personal drive and God's discernment cause extraordinary events, breakthroughs, or people?

Being born into a Eurasian family gave me strength and insight. My father revered the Japanese bushido tradition of living with honor in an everything-and-nothing reality. My Hungarian mother, influenced by the gypsies of her youth, believed in penetrating the unknown through clairvoyance within a God-centered universe.

Being born in 1938 and starting school shortly after the bombing of Pearl Harbor, I was condemned and ostracized as an American of Japanese descent, a factor which taught me to live in a world of day-to-day possibilities and to discover ways to survive and flourish.

Having dyslexia, a severe reading disability, and weak writing skills forced me to discover a creative approach to processing information, teaching me to delve more deeply into natural knowing.

God's intervention, the Holy Mother's blessing, Joshua's channeling, and a rich family tradition and seeking natural knowing combined to produce extraordinary, bordering-on-miraculous, experiences. The guiding voice or "whose voice is that," and repeated experiences of God's Divine Plan gave me lessons that resulted in a deep reservoir of creative processes and outcomes.

Chance or predestined meetings with mentors and organizations expanded my knowledge and helped me penetrate the unknown and unfathomable consciousness.

Learning to let go of pain, to disregard societal norms, and to love others, including my parents, just the way they are, or were, fostered in me The Space of Miracles and Samurai's Don't Cry and contributed to my being a Gypsy Samurai.

Life's purpose is about making a contribution to the lives of other people and always asking for permission to make that entry into their lives.

I thank God and his spiritual messengers.

I thank my wife for her generosity, her patience and her magic; she has sacrificed much that I might continue to learn and grow, supporting me when I was away in training programs, classes, and seminars in pursuit of degrees and certificates ad infinitum.

Ocha Deska (Tea Please)

My parents lived in a long, nine room railroad apartment in New York City, in the area now known as the Lincoln Center for the Performing Arts; our apartment actually overlooked Lincoln Center. My childhood parenting relationship was typified by my mother rocking in the east end of the apartment living room, always in a gingham dress and colorful, meticulously starched and perfectly appointed apron while my father was seated in the west end of the apartment kitchen, dressed in white underwear shorts, T-shirt with shoulder straps, eating toast and drinking coffee. He most often wore straw toe inset slippers or Japanese *setta*. This convenient seating arrangement placed them diametrically at the farthest ends of the apartment. Until 1945, when I was seven, my father was the more involved parent. In my later years when I was about six, my mother was the exclusive care-taker. My father jumped ship as a merchant marine upon entry into the United States; and through unconfirmed overheard conversations, he was a numbers runner in Chinatown.

The Ocha Deska experience was one that burned tradition and appropriate behavior with searing finality into my fingers, my sinews and my character. My father prepared tea (a very important and traditional Japanese ritual) in our kitchen with two of the boarders who lived with us. We seemed always to have at least one or two boarders that helped with family expenses: These two were Akira and Haruto. Akira was a retired aide of the United States Pacific Fleet. He was a family friend from a neighboring town adjacent to my father's home in Japan. Haruto was yet another close family friend whom my father new at least forty years. Their combined synergy equaled a complementary source of bonding by common language, traditions and anchored upon the issues that lived inside the conduct of having a long standing history of being the son of a past family and being Samurai with the Bushido tradition of conduct and traditional values. Without being brothers there became in time a bonded kinship. They were waiting for the ceremonial serving of excellent green Japanese tea, served in tea cups that were bulbously wide but short in height.

Unlike all other times, on this day I was invited to drink tea with them - a first and most auspicious occasion.

The tea had a distinctive, alluring aroma. My father sat at the head of the table; his two friends, as they came from his hometown, sat on his left. I directly faced my father, another unique experience since at dinner I always sat to his right and my mother faced him. The tea was poured into each cup with a slow calculated movement that seemed to extend time endlessly. Though the pouring spout seemed elongated not one drop was spilled other than being poured into the cradle of the respective cups. My cup was the last to be filled.

Jointly the cups were raised as if to celebrate an important occasion. The cup I held was scalding my tiny six year old hand. I can still recall the excruciating pain and shock as the degree of the heat being generated seared past my hand and touch my soul.

The cup held the heat impeccably. The toast was commemorated in a carefully worded Japanese statement by my father. The toast and tea ceremony was celebratory as well as extensive, as was the unbearable pain of holding that cup. I wanted to immediately drop the cup, but I held it as high as they did and prayed they would drink the tea quickly so that I could return the cup to the table.

I was clear I could not place my cup back on the table until they were the first to begin the motion. All I wanted was to drop the cup, but I continued to mimic them and held it high. I felt that my hand was melting - for sure they could see the flames of fire that engulfed my hand.

Yet even at the age of six, demonstrating appropriateness, calm, forbearance, showing "no effect" was paramount to this auspicious occasion, which was in my honor. They drew their cups graciously and solemnly to their mouths, I copied their actions, and in unison we drank. I was the first to bring my cup to rest on the table though they had started the downward motion and after a millisecond their cups followed in unison, landing on the table.

A tear welled up in my eyes and one quickly descended from my left eye which I quickly captured by a quick gesture as if rubbing my eyes. I hoped no one had seen this stealthy movement and it appeared no one had; but even if they had, such an acknowledgement was to be held as insuperable behavior. During this experience I attempted to create a counterpoint of pain by digging the fingers on my left hand as hard as I could into my left upper thigh: yet the burning of my right hand seemed more intense and at a higher level of penetration as time elapsed. My fear was that the pain would never abate and I would lose face by an inadvertent gesture or by dropping the cup. I recalled sitting there as if comatose, in a deep alpha state, attempting to cauterize the pain. My heart seemed it would explode; my brain was reeling, and my eyes became star ridden. I remember thinking, how can beings sustain this pain day after day?

They would drink tea periodically and so did I.

At one point my father glanced at me -- no, gazed at me -- and somehow I imagined he knew what I was going through. And maybe not, as one does not ask questions in Japanese traditional setting in such matters, so there is always the realm of uncertainty of what was so. Perhaps I made this all up about not asking questions. Since I never asked questions of my father, I will never know. In retrospect perhaps I created my own mysterious interactions and interventions, which meant I had importance and relevance. If nothing else I experience myself as Samurai and living the Bushido Code of Conduct.

At some point my father excused me from the table and he and his friends continued to speak in Japanese.

During the tea ceremony my father made a brief, barely audible toast: "Friendship is enriching when one holds onto

heated moments and enriching experiences without letting go."
My translation of what he said is most likely inaccurate, but it was
a close enough version and gave the experience some meaning in
terms of my interpretations of what was said.

Always, always experiences with my father were learning
experiences although they were relatively infrequent due to his
unavailability. Clearly there was a love – hate relationship that
existed all of my life toward my father. He set high standards
and expectations. In addition to my dyslexia my parents' very
separate lives and social ostracism during the Second World War
left me wandering and searching for some self evident truth of
who "I Am."

We need to Give You Away, Georgie

It always seemed to me that I was a good boy and seldom if ever did I cause any mischief or exhibit problematic behavior. It also seemed to me that others were attempting to damage me or kill me or violate me in some way. It always seemed as if my mother gave me assignments and there was never enough time to complete them before she returned to criticize the work as inadequate, wanting -- just not up to her standards. This was a double edged sword; living up to a code of conduct that did not take place within the culture and traditions of America and attempting to be 'good enough, fast enough, right enough or just barely, minimally enough'.

My mother often said to me, "Georgie, you know if you don't _____, I will need to give you away." Whenever she said this, I would always think what had I done wrong? I could never think of anything I was doing correctly. Although I was used to hearing she was going to give me away, one night I was more frightened than ever before.

One of our long-term boarders had a very beautiful woman as a 'friend.' Whenever Julie, the friend, would come over, they would close the door. This woman was full-figured, engaging and loving. When she came out of the room, she often spoke with my mother in the living room. One of these evenings, I entered the sitting room where they were talking. Once again, my mother said, "Georgie, you know if you don't _____, I will need to give you away." This was the first time she ever said this to me in front of another person. Her saying this in front of Julie made her words carry more meaning and I became very frightened. I did not know what I had done for her to say that. There were no incidents, disagreements, nor work I had not done. Then Julie leaned forward, turned toward me, and said, "You know your mother is telling you the truth. She will need to give you away; you need to listen to your mother."

I had known fear in the past, but Julie's words scorched my soul.

I was dying; death was present. I knew Julie would not express such an idea unless she felt it was true. Her affect, as I recall it, was serious; she seemed somewhat pained when she said it. Her usual compassion and kindness were missing. I think I asked Julie what I could do to not be thrown away, discarded. Julie said, "Just be a good boy, and do what your mother says." "But I am, I am, I don't do anything wrong." Maybe I said that or maybe I just thought it. My world fell away and fell apart. If my mother gave me away, when I was only eight or nine, the world out there would kill me and no one would ever know what happened to me. The world out there was hostile and belligerent and only in remaining home was there some hope of avoiding engaging with the enemy who lived everywhere. I would be fair game.

I knew that good Japanese soldiers do not cry, but I was terrified and I began to cry and begged not to be given away. I started to become hysterical, and I remember I wanted to jump out of the window only a few feet away. I don't recall ever being in such a panic. At that moment Julie got up and looked at my mother and said, "Georgie, if necessary I will take you." My mother seemed incredulous, confused and angry. I don't recall what occurred next, for I collapsed. No one ever again spoke of giving me away, yet the lingering fear was always a close reality.

In the months that followed I had horrifying nightmares. I would lie in my bed and hear loud noises. The sounds became louder and louder and I'd begin to sink as if I were starting to slide down a spiraling corridor of space. The sounds became deafening and I fought not to fall into this vortex of abandonment and helplessness. Once there, I knew I could never return. Night after night this dreadful experience reoccurred and I told no one. I was sure if I told my mother, she would get rid of me and I could not let that happen. I would fight going to sleep as long as I could, but the inevitable droning sound and spiraling would begin. When, or how or why this experience disappeared remains a mystery.

One evening I simply fell asleep and the nightmare did not return.

Once I recalled an experience of drowning in a river in Perth Amboy, New Jersey and I was saved by an adolescent swimming nearby. I was going under the water line and churning and twisting in the quiet and still river and someone saved me. I used every ounce of my energy to remain in control.

I had thought that perhaps if I slipped under someone would have come to save me, but I could not imagine who that would have been.

The war had been over for just one year and men were returning home from the South Pacific. Families in the axis power neighborhood I lived in shared stories with tales of an unsavory adversary; they told of buck-toothed, slanty eyed yellow men, the Japs, sneaky and treacherous, raping and pillaging, with values from an unsavory culture, not the one you and I live in. I needed to run home, constantly looking over my shoulder on the streets not to be beaten or captured and tortured in basements. There were infrequent entrapments in basements, and I had good probable cause for being on constant watch.

On two occasions I distinctly recall being befriended and invited into a lair [basement] where clubs and meetings were held among the neighborhood youth. I was then abducted, captured, held against my will, and threatened with bodily harm. The more serious of these two incidents was when I was dragged into a basement room and the superintendent's son conducted a formal tribunal. Most of the children in the neighborhood had gathered and a hearing was conducted to determine my fate. I was shunted into a corner, sitting on top of boxes several feet high looking down over the assembly. I was frightened as this group appeared serious and whatever their sentence was to be, it appeared ominous; and whatever the outcome, it felt tragic and menacing. The meeting seemed to proceed slowly with threats, scowls, jeering, yelling and calling for diabolical actions such as "give him a beating of a lifetime," "kick his eyes out," "everyone stab him once and see if he likes how it feels," and name calling of every variety. My mind was whirling and I felt light headed and wanted to run. But then where could I run? The door was quite a distance away from where the main body of assailants sat and stood in judgment. The superintendent's father coincidentally entered the room, questioned his son and others about what was going on and looking toward the far corner of the basement room saw me cowering, seated on some boxes. The children seemed concerned and anxious. As he approached me several of the children left the room. "George, why are you sitting in the corner like that?" I remained silent for I knew in the aftermath of this tribunal anything I said would be held against me and I would assuredly be punished severely. He sensed my fear and the dilemma and asked me to come down to where he was standing. By this time almost everyone in the room had left other than his son and his closest friends. I realized his father who was known as a strict disciplinarian would punish his son and I feared future retaliation which for some reason never occurred, though I waited from day to day to be captured again and to be tortured and beaten.

Teachers who said, "GO BACK TO JAPAN WHERE YOU CAME FROM" didn't even know I was never in Japan. "God, God, please don't let me slip into that abyss again." I always prayed to God to save me from this horrible castigating world. There was one time when I went up to the roof and stood on the edge. I wanted to jump; the circumstances that day had been unbearable, but at the last minute a voice, probably of my own making said, "Come from this place, my son. I will be with you forever and you will not be alone again."

"Was that my voice?" Was it simple fear of not wanting to jump from the sixth floor? Whose voice was that? "Thank you, God, for giving me such an extraordinary life experience for living through this historical nightmare."

It has forged a diamond's diamond; and in that light I will serve others less fortunate; for I have lived in the darkest places imaginable and Thou has been at my side, for Thy love comforts me and makes me whole." I know 'You" are there for "You" have always been there; there is no presence other than your presence.

Torture the Jap: Slap Him, Slap Him, Get Him, Get Him Now

Nevertheless, I was still an animal that was captured on the street, even though I ran away and was usually slapped and spat upon on top of a hood of a car (no further than one block from my grade school), and then when I slumped down on the ground the perpetrator would release me, cursing and laughing.

There was one student in particular, Herbie, who actually lived on the opposite side of street from me, who would most often engage in this aggressive behavior. My worst nightmare was being befriended or at least it seemed so, invited into some basement or clubroom and then trapped and tortured by students that I would and did sit next to at school.

Like a white rabbit, I was fair game in any season. A strategy that was particularly crafty and cunning was fixing a calligraphy pen [nib inserted into a pen holder] into a school briefcase which was common in those days, walking behind me and stabbing me from behind in my lower calf muscle. This usually occurred at the end of the school day when I was ready to leave for home. Even through I had periscope up at 360 degrees, the marauders moved swiftly and with great stealth; they worked in teams to maneuver their crafty game plan.

Countless times I and my mother would visit our family doctor who would swab the area and take some other precautions. The wait times seemed interminable and there was minimal to no conversation between me and my mother as we waited for the doctor in the vestibule of his building; he seemed never to be in the office when we dropped by.

Strange, on those occasions it seemed always to be raining heavily and I was wearing a large black rain hat and raincoat, the kind that had those shiny metal snaps. My internal dialogue was active with thoughts of why I was such a target to be invalidated, tortured, stabbed, spat upon and treated as not only the unwanted, but despised for the Second World War which I was innocent of; I had nothing to do with it. During each of those medical visits I would be medically treated and thought some other major medical issue would be a tragic outcome. My mother never ever seemed to give me words of consolation or how to understand the anger that surrounded me everywhere; she was stoic, resolute, proud, a force of nature to be reckoned with. Her resolve to be married to a native born Japanese man never speaking of any issues or personal concerns were perhaps the same resolve or resoluteness she shared in her experience with me. As I reflect back, in later life, I never asked her qualifying questions, "Good Japanese soldiers don't ask questions - they follow orders unquestioningly". My mother shared a story with me, perhaps one of the few, which was when she married my father at City Hall, New York City, the respective couples lined up two by two and approached a white line and a city official. The official beckoned to my mother only to approach and to sit down beside him. He leaned toward my mother and asked if she was going to marry "that man" who stood alone waiting to advance, this probably occurred several years after I was born. My mother who was in her early of mid forties said yes with a heavy Hungarian accent which was always a distinctive characteristic until she died at the age of 99 ½ at a Residential Care Center in upstate New York, 1998. The man then said, "You know those people don't have blood like you and me." My mother asked "what kind of blood do they have". To which he responded "yellow blood". My mother with perhaps a 9th grade education returned to the line with my father and said "mister you do your job now". That was the character and strength of my mother - resolute and proud.

I don't recall what was said by my mother or the doctor.

Call of the Wild by Jack London

School was always a challenge when I lived with my parents. Reading especially was a difficult & harrowing experience; as hours would go by and it would seem I had only read one page or two, with hundreds yet to be read. I read so slowly and at times my thinking wandered so that what I read was empty and meaningless. What seemed important was to keep reading. However, what was said, who had done what, what actions had taken place remained a complete mystery to me.

I was absolutely determined to complete *The Call of the Wild*, by Jack London, no matter what. I recall lying on the floor in the living room, in my parent's railroad apartment, reading for an indeterminable period of time. It was getting dark outside and my mother was rocking in her favorite chair. She asked me what I was reading and I said something like, "It's a book required by Ms. DeForte for English." I knew if I didn't learn how to read my ability to function in this world would be limited if not completely unavailable.

More time went by and I was swirling, cascading down, lost and going no where, knowing nothing, wondering if this experience would ever change. My mother said, "Georgie, if you are having trouble, why don't you stop?" What I heard was, "It's hopeless; give up," rather than a supportive statement like "Take a break and come back to the reading assignment." At that moment I felt defeated. I wanted to burn the book and jump out of life and disappear. Without my mother's support, patience and encouragement, even if she could not read or write English and neither could my father how could I manage this unbearable experience? I hated myself, my mother and education.

I believe at that moment I wanted to die; life was hopeless. I don't think I ever finished reading a book throughout public school, although given that I'm remembering back over 65 years, maybe this observation is inaccurate. Maybe I read several books, or parts of books. Education at that time meant students moved along from grade to grade in keeping with their chronological ages. I was good. I did my chores. I loved God and people. Why was it so difficult for me to learn or study? I seemed to have no ability to remember things. I was always anxious in school. One good thing was that no teacher ever called on me recite or answer questions except once. I'll never ever forget that one time Mrs. Sullivan called on me in the third grade. As I stood up, expecting her to ask me to recite a lesson I had not prepared for and that I could not read, she said at the top of her voice, "Why don't you go back to Japan where you came from?" Life closed down at that moment. There was no tomorrow, no future, no love; no one wanted me; I was to be destroyed and discarded.

"God, what have I done to deserve this?" I had no one to share my pain with. Good Japanese soldiers cannot share their fear or pain; they must bear life's pain and suffering, ask no quarter and take no quarter, there were no out stretched hands and guides to make a difference.

And so life went on. I quickly discovered that people enjoyed those who were funny and playful, so I attempted to hide my pain and avoid their enmity by inventing a playful act or skit, or being funny, ridiculous, and outrageous. In this state of "being George," people seemed less apt to want to hurt or humiliate me; they wanted another wondrous antic, another comical act and this was a new persona to hide from persecution.

Meet your enemy before they can engage you and they will sometimes forget their intended volley of righteous indignation. Hiding in such a framework separates you from others, for the shield in time hardens into armor that keeps people out and makes you invisible even to yourself.

The act becomes all there is.

Perhaps the pain is hidden, perhaps you're safe, but your life is still brewing its seeds of discontent, shame, blame and feelings of inadequacy.

Mother Son Rite of Passage

My mother had sent me to a summer camp that was part of our church in at the age of thirteen. It was for two August weeks in upstate New York. Several of us arrived by bus and were quickly ushered to our respective rooms. I was very frightened by these new surroundings and worried about whether I would be accepted in this new environment. I was always scared of people's reactions and craved their acceptance, and not to be hurt.

At the end of the first week I received a care package from my mother and I felt remembered and loved. I shared the food and other goodies with my roommate.

Our room was far removed from the principal barrack-like housing, but it was adequate and the screened-in porch was warm and cozy. I did wonder why he and I were separated from the main group of children that seemed to live in a common barrack setting. We were the only ones coupled together and set apart some distance from the other boys that slept in dormitory style housing. Perhaps the other boy who was black and I were to be kept apart from general housing. Only in writing this book has the issue of separation ever been an observable issue; at the time it just seemed we were being provided with special housing accommodations.

I recall having to leave camp before my two weeks elapsed because I had two substantial bite marks on my upper inside left thigh. I was running a fever and felt mildly nauseous. Once I was back home, the doctor came to see me on an almost daily basis. My mother was very upset about my health, which continued to decline. My principal complaint was feeling hot, and an infection had set in and the bite marks were festering. The doctor said if the fever did not go down I would need to be hospitalized. My impression was that the two marks set close together looked like a snake bite, but was my imagination making up stories or not.

My mother told me that we needed to work very closely together and that I needed to follow her instructions very carefully. She never said why we were doing this, but I knew that her exposure to the gypsies who used to visit her family in Hungary played a very large part in her spiritual beliefs. She asked me to: locate a four-way cross roads of my choosing; say specific words in Hungarian; not look as I crossed the roadway; face south, and throw a silver coin over my left shoulder repeating the incantation, then keep walking, and not watch where the coin dropped.

I was very frightened, but I followed all of her directions impeccably except one. Cars were moving south and I could have been hit by oncoming vehicular traffic, so I did peek quickly to avoid being hit by an oncoming car. Looking back, I realize that had my mother looked out of our window she would have seen exactly what actions I followed in her rituals since our apartment window faced that avenue.

By the next day all physical signs and symptoms had disappeared as if they were never there; both my fever and the puncture marks were gone. We never spoke of the meaning of the ritual and I never questioned the meaning of the words I'd spoken. She did use a compost mixture on the wound which was a remedy she undoubtedly learned from the gypsies she frequented. My life was always accepting what my parents said without question.

My parents met in Connecticut both working as domestics. My mother was a house keeper while my father was the family cook and at times the chauffeur.

My mother knew about healing herbs and remedies. She used to say that she needed to be careful not to get angry or to curse someone in a certain way or terrible things would befall that person. I noticed she would call back some angry outbursts and say certain things in her native language. She said that once she invoked certain forces, those forces could not be called back. She reported that gypsies were always in close proximity to her parents' home and I believe they may actually have lived on their land. Her father was a contractor, who owned livestock, sold meat and was prominent and respected in her community in Hungary, living in Buda. She reported that her parents were people of means, and that she could speak several languages, among them Hungarian, German and Yiddish. She said that on certain days of the week Jewish people would come to collect bread her parents made, and that on Fridays, rabbis would come to their home to converse. I later learned that only Jewish people made their holy bread, and no Jew would buy such bread from a gentile, did that make her Jewish I have absolutely no idea, though her religious beliefs were clearly Christian.

When she left Hungary her family was experiencing great difficulty with communism. Relatively early in her life her father was killed in a fire when a beam struck him on his head. Her brother was apparently killed by the Russians. She and her sister came to the United States at different times, but in relatively close proximity. My mother sailed from Cherbourg and arrived in the United States on October 16, 1925. She reported her birth date as August 20, 1898. While traveling by steamer to the United States, she befriended a woman on board who taught her to read Tarot cards, and she became a very accomplished and notable New York tarot card reader. She could read and write in her own language but not in English. She was extraordinarily gifted in her clairvoyance. My understanding is that she never became a citizen of the United States, though my father became a naturalized citizen on May 26, 1958.

I believe there may have been a time that my mother separated from my father, probably when I was an infant, but she repeatedly informed me that she stayed with my father all those years only to provide a home for me, and would have left him if I had not been born. Because of her limitations with the English language and few skills, economically she may have needed to remain with my father as many women in a similar plight need to compromise the best for themselves and their offspring. Because of this, and because of my father's customary angry outbursts, I tended to align with my mother against my father. My relationship with my father was distant, strained, angry, avoidant and filled with conflict and detached isolation. My relationship with my mother was a love-hate one. It was my experience that my mother was always a housewife and never worked after I was born. My parents met as domestic workers employed by a wealthy family in Connecticut. When she made a commitment to live with my father, her wealthy New England relatives ended their relationship with her. Only her elder sister Frieda who lived in Monroe, New Jersey, remained in limited contact. On two to three occasions she took me to visit Frieda's family, but those visits were brief and she reported she couldn't wait to get back home.

My mother was very progressive. She brought me to The Ethical Culture School in New York as part of their recreational center while attending public high school, took me to Central Park to attend music concerts on a regular basis during the summer months, and was particularly interested in classical movies such as Hamlet and Macbeth, and especially religious movies like "The Ten Commandments."

She died just four months shy of her one hundredth birthday, on April 20, 1999, in Margaretville, in the Catskills of New York.

Samurai's Don't Cry

I can still hear the clickety-click of the Sea Beach subway heading to Coney Island, Brooklyn, home of the Dodgers: they left home and so did I. Our trip to Brooklyn was one of the very few occasions we spent time together as a family. There appeared to be a thousand quiet penetrating stares of wonderment from passengers on that train. It was 1948 and I was ten years old. I sat with my mother while my father sat alone. Theirs was an inter-racial marriage. My father came from a southern province in Japan, Fukuoka-Ken, while my mother came from Hungary's capital, the Buda side of Budapest. Station after station people entered or exited on a ride that seemed almost endless, yet the sign read "Coney Island" and I knew it was the last stop. The people disembarking looked like single giant bodies snaking through a long corridor, doing a very slow to and fro shuffle changing form at random one station after another. When the train stopped at our station, throngs of people moved downward in a sloping, to me galloping, spiral toward the street level.

We moved steadily southward, street after street, toward the parakeet man. Mr. Abe had a welcoming smile and was perhaps in his early seventies. He said, "You have a handsome son Tani-san." My father replied, "Asodeska?" [Is that so?] My plummeting sense of self-worth was reflected by my downcast eyes and demeanor as my father said, "He is ugly and dumb." In Japanese culture such a demeaning response was commonplace and was said by one's father to prevent too heightened a sense of self-worth by one's children. Mr. Abe, however, seemed to sense my shame and despair and perhaps recognized his responsibility in raising an issue which was sensitive to me. At his prompting a parakeet hopped up a tiny ladder which acted as a roadway to a large pile of miniature pink scrolls, extracted one and hopped back and dropped the scroll into a box. Like a Chinese fortune cookie the message read, "Faith is a power that changes the course of one's destiny." The question, "What exactly did the last word mean?" lingered in my mind.

We seemed to walk endlessly farther and farther south past almost every numbered bay, well beyond the parachute jump which was barely visible. I never addressed or questioned my father's word. The way it was, was the way it was, final and binding, but I wondered when we would get to stop. It was almost noon when we finally put our blanket down and I quickly stretched out to bask in the sun.

Several hours later I was playing at the edge of the water, fearing the water since I could not swim. The waves were breaking ominously, crashing with a thunderous bang as if the ground beneath the wave was being cracked and torn apart. My father invited me to join him in the water and assured me we would only go wading and I knew that some dreadful experience awaited me, though I had no idea it would not be the tide or the cascading waves that would terrify me. The water was icy and grew even colder the farther out we went. He held me facing the beach as he paddled out farther and farther into the sea. I was terrified that I would disappear beneath the dark waters. My grip tightened and, though fear and trembling was unacceptable for a Samurai's son, he quietly reassured me, "I'm a good swimmer, don't worry." The current and his backward stroke pulled us farther and farther out of sight of the people on the beach, and umbrellas and the boardwalk became so small at one point I could no longer see them, the shore or the people wading and swimming. My fear was at a perilous level, but Samurais do not cry, nor do they show fear, nor ask for help.

At that moment I vaguely remember my father saying, "In life there will be times when you cannot see the shore, but you know it's there. In such times only your belief in yourself will bring you the strength you need." I wanted to thrash about and scream and pull away and say, "I can't swim, please go back," but such a request was clearly not appropriate, not the Japanese way. This was one of the many object lessons that comprised my mentoring. I felt I was being frozen in ice and my body hurt. Farther and farther he swam, perhaps unaware that I was terrified or building an inner strength to live courageous, miraculously; living outside the box of fear and trembling. I was lost in an internal screaming silence...every aspect of my being cried to end this death experience.

Finally, he turned and began to swim back, and I swore if I got to shore I would never go anywhere with him again.

When we reached the beach my mother had a towel and there were angry words between the two of them, words which for me were muted out. My mother wiped me off as I stood shivering, disoriented and dismayed. There was a large gathering of people assembled around us, including a life guard.

My father remembered an earlier incident and proceeded to tell me that story. He began talking about once when he was drowning, going down for the third time when a lifeguard reached him and saved his life.

He said the lifeguard later questioned him, "Do you know that area was off limits," and my father replied, "I know the current is strong and difficult." The lifeguard said in all his years he had never had such an experience: "You placed your hand upon my shoulder and helped me save your life, yet you were going down for the third time, did you know that?" My father said he was aware he was drowning.

The life-guard went on to say, "How is it possible for you to reach out to support me -- not grab onto me? Weren't your frightened?" My father said, "If I were frightened, nothing you did or could have done would have saved your life or mine. Knowing that, it was best to save your life, not mine."

He then told me a second story.

As a quartermaster in the merchant marines, he had developed skills as a long distance swimmer. While he was on a ship and with another worker were painting the ship. There was a section his shipmate could not reach so he sat on my father's shoulders and shortly thereafter there was an explosion. Steam filleted the skin off my father's legs. My father explained that had he at that moment collapsed or fallen, his shipmate would have fallen to his death. My father waited for his partner to dismount from his shoulders before he was taken to the infirmary in excruciating pain. The captain asked him how it was possible to be scalded, with skin peeling off his legs, yet hold his ground, "How did you do that?" My father answered, "In life there are times one must be still, to go beyond pain in order to save another's life. This is the training of being a Samurai."

Such training had been indoctrinated in him by his family traditions, training and mentoring. He went on to say, "One must always expect the unexpected. Therefore, it becomes the expected outcome and not out of one's control. Outcomes in life are probable, certain and to be expected if one is prepared to accept the impossible."

I did not ask any questions about these two stories, just simply attempted to internalize their meanings. To demonstrate bravery, courage and stamina, to overcome pain and fear of the unknown, to protect life and property, to be committed to a higher order of achievement by selflessness were the traditional values I grew up with.

I first wrote of the Coney Island experience on June 18, 1989, and when I read it to my mother the following day, she said, "It's a wonderful long story, George. Your father seems always to swim in deep waters, teaching you difficult lessons in life. Those lessons make you challenge yourself to find your inner strength."

Snow Feet to the Mountain and Back

―――――――――――――――― ⚬ ――――――――――――――――

The winter of 1948 was one of coldest in forty years.

My mother was hospitalized and my father was working for a family in Connecticut and it was difficult or impossible for me to stay with him. I was sent to my godmother, Rosemary, that winter, for a period of two or three months. My father seldom called and my mother was too ill to communicate.

During this period of time I was isolated from all that was familiar and this period of time in Bradley Gardens, New Jersey, seemed an eternity. My godmother was of German heritage, and though American born, she was autocratic, demanding and extraordinarily strict. Feelings seemed to me to be portioned out like the last cup of water in a desolate lost horizon township in the Sahara. My godfather, John, worked at the local Sherman Williams Paint Company. While he seemed distant, my being respectful and doing a good job appeared to meet his criteria of my being a good boy, and, therefore, earned me some peaceful acceptance.

Auntie Ro, as I called her, was totally unwilling to accept that I was dyslexic and, consequently, I experienced grueling "school" sessions since I had great difficulty reading, spelling and remembering. To me it was just like James Cagney in Strasse 29 being interrogated by the SS just before the American forces bombed the headquarters of the Gestapo. She relentlessly asked me question after question, hour after hour of my 'trying' to remember and holding back the tears because Japanese soldiers do not cry, not under any circumstances. Standing in front of her, not even seated, I failed abysmally.

As the months passed there seemed to be less attention to learning my ABC's. I recall that when I was in the second grade in 1945, my father had prepared a crib sheet on how to bring letters together. While I was using this reference, my home room teacher, Mrs. Ryan, found the paper and held the tell tale document high into the air and said, "We have one person in this room that can't even spell - shameful, shameful, shameful." That was that. Everyone knew I was dumb, just as my father would say validating my learning limitations. I had to remind myself: "Remember Georgie - one never surrenders; there is no loss unless you say so, and the struggle is to overcome adversity and to excel toward greatness no matter what obstacles are in one's path."

I waited for each snowfall as if determining when to go on my mission, though I don't think I called it that or knew it to be that. At the time waiting for a blizzard seemed as if it was an idea whose time would and had come.

It was early in the morning and I knew it was time to go on this journey into nowhere. I bundled up. I remember my galoshes which were black with large silver snaps, three or four as I recall, that could snap shut. I also placed some wax paper between the galoshes and my winter socks. I recollect Auntie Ro asked me, "Where are you going so early this morning?" My comment was "Just to play in the snow" or something like that, simple and to the point. She warned me not to stray too far, not to go into the adjacent forest and to come back soon. I agreed, though I knew I would not come back until my mission, as I call it now, was complete.

My agreement with myself was to walk as far as I could go, without paying attention to direction, and only when I was exhausted would I turn around to attempt the trip back. I remember that when I reached the edge of the woods (about two and a half blocks away in a very underdeveloped area at that time in New Jersey), the snow was just at my boot line, before it reached my pants.

On and on I trudged, tree after tree, field after open field, heavily wooded forest after forest. At one point I followed deer tracks, and at another point I saw a buck and two does hurrying along a path. A white tailed rabbit darted out in front of me and I was saddened since I did not have my bee-bee gun, not realizing one bee-bee or two would have made no meaningful impact.

My thighs were aching, burning and I was sweating profusely. I was stopping frequently to catch an extra breath and sometimes to try to get my bearing. Clearly, I was lost. The terrain and surroundings were totally foreign to me, and nothing looked even remotely familiar. About four hours after I had started, I knew I was completely lost in a densely wooded foreign forest, and clearly challenged by the elements.

The snow had stopped for a brief period and when it began again, it felt as if I was walking into walls of snow. I remember falling face down in the snow. I don't recall if it was exhaustion or just taking in a new experience. It never dawned on me why I had embarked on this mission; it just seemed the time to do it was now. The sky was gray and ominous.

I experienced little fear on the outward journey; however, the voyage back clearly became a question of "Will I make it?" I could not feel my feet. They were damp and I was wet, but not soaking, from the perspiration; nevertheless, I was dressed warmly. It dawned on me that perhaps I should have taken some food; and being thirsty, the melted snow tasted good.

It was getting darker; night was descending quickly, and it was many miles back to the farmhouse on the edge of the forest. On and on and on I trudged. From time to time I thought I heard my name in the distance, but then I thought this was just my overactive imagination. Darkness was closing in all around me. My legs felt like two huge boulders that I was dragging. I could hear my heartbeat pounding in my head and throughout my body and I experienced fatigue, which was new to me since I had tremendous strength. (The Tani genetic strain was known for incredible strength - I had to stop wiping any drinking glasses many years back as I would most often snap the glass.) I had heard of frostbite, but clearly I had no idea what frostbite meant, felt or looked like.

I glanced to my immediate left and saw a lean-to which was covered with a sheet of snow. I remember trying to raise myself onto the extremely slippery, wet surface. It was like scaling a rock precipice. In time I managed to reach the top and centered myself on the oblique surface, sliding just several inches from the bottom. I lay there trying to regain my energy. Strangely, I was not shivering. But subsequently I felt cold in my extremities and then I did start to shiver. I forced myself to relax and after fifteen or twenty minutes, I heard my name being called out in the distance and realized that people were looking for me. I saw one figure through the trees some great distance away on a knoll, but my extremities were becoming covered with snow.

I hoped against hope that they would see me and at the same time I prayed that I might finish this experience by myself. I don't know why I did not call out; perhaps I did and didn't realize it. I had no name for this happening; event or journey, other than it was some rite of passage.

The Emergence of the
Clairvoyant and Clairsentient

The emergence or breakthrough of being clairvoyant and clairsentient happened at different times. As a child foretelling the future seemed like visualizing events that did not necessarily fit existing life experiences; most such occurrences happened around the age of nine, but were not fully matched with actual life experiences between the ages of fifteen to eighteen as déjà vu. Distinguishing the two realities seemed to merge into one another as normal adaptive functioning with little inquisitiveness or alarm.

As a child, living directly across the later construction of the Lincoln Center for the Performing Arts, a conundrum was why I could not pass my hand into a wall and then withdraw it, though I knew solids were not penetrable unless by a major force of energy assuredly not a hand, yet why couldn't I make it happen. This was an inquiry being an only child, reclusive and isolated from other children afforded me time to ponder and visualize an internal imagining of an improbable visualization.

Countless experiences facilitated my engaging in stretching my imagination of the possibility of extraordinary outcomes. If one holds the vision of a dream in time it becomes not only a reality but a stepping stone of other remarkable stepping stones or as Buddha said, "what we think we become".

An internal voice was very complimentary, like a guiding light in the storm and the quiet sailing of my mind, always seemingly directing me; this voice took time to cultivate and integrate, yet it was always a presence which clearly seemed to be a wishing to create a separate world of reality and contribution.

My father's bushido tradition of honor, integrity, fearlessness and stories of valor and self-determination and my mother's special psychic powers to predict happenings at times with her tarot cards, incantations and spells facilitated my clairvoyance. Her strength and conviction about what was right and just and making a difference in contributing to people's lives by her generosity and insights of listening, guiding, foretelling cradled and nurtured a powerful resource that miraculous ways of contributing are possible.

The Second World War ended when I was seven years old. Being Eurasian and living in New York City struggling to overcome America's pain and anger toward the atrocity of Pearl Harbor's atrocity which engendered intolerance and prejudice. Relocation camps for Japanese Americans was an imagined safeguard to protect internal insurrection, but since my mother was Hungarian and since we lived in the Northeast and since most detainees were principally from the West Coast and adjoining states, it was necessary to develop greater wisdom and perception of people, places and things to find a safe harbor from being severely harmed or killed. Having severe learning disorder dyslexia also forced me to find a reality that could help me cope and function in grade school.

While my parents were struggling and challenged to adapt to two diametrically divergent cultures, it appeared to me that the principle belief was a hands off policy both in outcomes at school of stabbings, beatings and name calling and not being advocates to assist me with school educators with the inhumane way children were reacting to me. Entering the school each day during those early years was with a sense of doom and foreboding for my well-being and avoiding being caught without other people being around could potentially result in disastrous outcomes. My perennial sense was there was no one out there to protect me and that each day might be the last day of my life. The hardest part of the day was entering the school. I always seemed to be late rushing to class; when you're late customarily there is no one behind you.

It seemed necessary to surrender, to forgive unjust reactions of beatings, stabbings, being spat upon and chased home from school and near death experiences trapped by my contemporaries in basements, shallow and abysmal bonding with classmates or neighborhood children seemed to create a fertile environment to seek the extraordinary, the miraculous, possibility and develop a rich imagination and creative energy to invent a new world of reality, one that I could live and survive in.

My mother had a deep and committed relationship with God and that while her guiding statements "that sticks and stones may break my bones, names will never harm me" she as well was a gifted psychic medium of seeing life unfold for others before their time. She was always being creative and generating culture, music and opportunities for me to be more fully expressed as someone approaching a renaissance man. She would bring me to revival meetings and those events sparkled of people being touched by the Holy Spirit and uplifted. As we sat in box seats on the second floor, women in the orchestra directly below us were being transported by the holy spirit in what seemed to be not only out of body experiences but being touched by the spirit of God in some euphoric expression; I sensed that "God was good and God was great" and present to reach out and touch, inspire and anoint my soul to transcend. While, unlike these inspired women of God I was transported to a space and essence of a higher power that was present regardless of whether I could see God as they did or not, he was ever present everywhere. Perhaps this experience was a fantasy; but the reality it created was affirming, uplifting and provided a redeemer from the inhuman cruelty in my day to day life experience.

I was always far sighted in my natural knowing that I should go to a Catholic High School because of their mentoring programs to assist my learning disorder, or selling eggs and chickens from my God-mother's farm to earn money and to provide benefits to my community that the war years had made more challenging to purchase, or selling Christmas Cards and greeting cards during holiday seasons or during Halloween choosing a location and costume, and some incredulous story that would create as much as twenty dollars in one night trick or treating when a nickel was an extra-ordinary way of gifting anyone. All this was possible in

1947 to 1950 from the ages of 9 to 11, just before puberty. It was also a way of experiencing people I never met before, engaging them, being myself and generating a relationship and relatedness to others and discovering their essence that brought them joy and happiness and acceptance to be me. The costume I wore masked my oriental features and gave me more freedom of self expression.

While apprenticing for a creative communication corporation in 1980 some amazing breakthroughs in working with families, couples and individuals occurred. There were fifteen executives who were part of a workshop held over four months whose purpose was to help people achieve results in career, primary relationship and family as well as prosperity and specific outcomes possible not in the domain of one of the areas already cited. There always seemed to be a corridor or entry way and intuition how to engage the executives and their families that lead to extraordinary and acclaimed outcomes and solutions. What I remember most in my second year of doing such work was people saying "did you see that" and their expressions were filled with awe and wonderment and I was able to take this in within a range of 1 to 10, as a 2 and possible 3, 10 being great excitation about their realization and breakthrough or self acceptance.

Being clairsentient occurred substantially later in a series of sequential experiences. One such experience was at Markim Beverages. While being the manager a co-worker walked into my offices and some fifteen to eighteen feet away while he was approaching me I said, "How is your cold doing". He entered the room and responded, "How do you know I have a cold?" He said that I could not have seen his eyes from that distance. I indicated

I had studied iridology while attending the Center of the Light in Great Barrington, Massachusetts [Graduated on August 25, 1983] the Training of Healers a two year program. That I knew about iridology comprehensively was not true but I needed to make up a story of how I knew when in fact I had no idea in order not to appear strange, weird and questionably a person to report to senior management as strange. I quickly changed the subject to the work I had done at the Center. As George Bernard Shaw said, "Life isn't about finding yourself. Life is about creating yourself."

Another breakthrough story occurred on Long Beach Island where my wife and I had been summer renters for almost some nineteen years. I was invited to the home of Linda and Michael Cella, by his wife to do a body reading for her husband; this also occurred during the time I was at the Center of the Light at Great Barrington. When I arrived it was like a test for me, yet I was not nervous or uncertain of my abilities; there was one twinge when I walked down Ocean Road on Long Beach Island, "who am I to do such a body reading without receiving information beforehand". The reading was very successful and it was then that he said he was a lawyer from Long Island. That set off all kinds of bells and whistles as we needed as a healing group to be mindful of claims of the laying on of hands or such mystical powers as the medical profession maintained laws and practices which made such overt behavior, that is the laying on of hands which did not occur during our one hour session, probable. My mind was running rampant. Nevertheless, I had misgivings about my reading and was assured that what my observations were not illegal and an extraordinary gift to be offered to others. The question arises why aren't we magicians? Luke Skywalker, upon seeing Yoda lift his X-wing fighter out of the swamp using only his mind: I don't believe it! Yoda: And that is why you fail.

A third story was while I was in Westchester, New York. A Jungian Center, I was a member of their Board of Directors most closely approximating 1981. The minister met with me first before I met with the President and his administrative executive committee concerning contributions that I wanted to make with regard to building enhancements and more economical use of electrical energy at their facility as I had brought a support group to contribute their expertise pro bono. I made many statements concerning what I call my natural knowing and insights. The minister as I recall was a graduate from an Ivy League Divinity school who said, "While I have never met someone like you, such people are called Messengers of God, but I am sure you know this." To me this claim was a strange and unknown harbinger of experiences to come and not until many years later was there a true understanding of this biblical expression.

I found a statement by Joe Dispenza in the book What the Bleep do We know!? Pg. 233,

"What is the definition of any miracle? Something that happens outside of convention, outside the box of what's socially acceptable, scientifically acceptable, religiously acceptable, and right outside the box is where human potential exists. How do we get there? We have to overcome the emotional states that we live in on an everyday basis. Our own personal doubt, our own feelings of unworthiness, our own lethargy and historically borrowed doubts and fears impregnate our growth." Our own voices that say we're not good enough or it's impossible are the listening channels that trap our greatness of expression and creativity. The voices in the distance as well as the figure trailed off and I realized that if I did not acknowledge myself to the "posse" I could die. Some part of me wanted to die, some part of me wanted to live and the challenge was there for me to complete. The snow flakes were the largest I had ever seen; the quiet was pervasive and empowering. That very moment was one of the sweetest of my life. There were snow banks all over and I became afraid, a fear that I had never even experienced in school. Why had I done this? What was I trying to prove? No one I knew did such a thing or maybe they just never shared that experience as it was too personal. I also knew my godmother would be extremely angry and I would be severely punished and beaten. At that moment I feared that beating as if it were already happening to me. The idea of being beaten occurred several times in a periodic cluster and then disappeared.

I tried to move and my body was rigid and fixed as if I was the bark on a tree being held in position by the supporting surface of the earth that had temporarily lifted its face to see itself at another angle. When my feet touched the surface of the ground, they would not support me. All I felt were pins and needles shooting across every facet of my feet as if someone was exploding dynamite, blasting and ricocheting everywhere. I fell forward. I could not walk or even stand. It was no longer a matter of being just cold, wet, frozen and maybe frost bitten. My body would not respond to my commands. I was confused, scared and I thought of dying right there.

I gathered my courage, went deep into the centrality of mind, and began to crawl. Crawling was slow; an inch seemed as if time was standing still. I knew I had to stand and to gain control of my body, no matter how extreme the pain. Slowly, gradually I made it to my feet. Inch by inch and yard by yard I moved in the direction where I heard my name, calling for someone to help me. I avoided the snow banks and kept creeping forward. The pain was unbearable from time to time, and so what. On and on I went. By now it was at least one-half hour or so before complete darkness covered the tree line. I saw in the distance what appeared to be a familiar clearing close to where I had begun my journey. I did not know if I was dreaming or just making this up or if this was just a mirage.

I then contemplated the most frightening thought: When I cleared the wood line, who would see me and what would my godmother do to me? She was in the driveway as I inched forward. I was both glad to see her and very frightened about the consequences of my actions.

The moment she saw me she started screaming at me and running: "He's alive, he's alive. John - J, he's alive." It was incredible; she was up the driveway and at my side before I recall taking even another step. At first she hugged me and then she was asking me what seemed like a dozen funny questions: "Has someone abducted you?" "Where did you go?" "Didn't you hear the posse?" I remained silent for I did not want to lie and had to think about what in fact was my truth. I had been taught always to tell the truth, yet I was not sure what the truth was and why had I gone so far and come so close to death and dying. Was I insane? Did I really want to kill myself?

Shortly thereafter I was slapped in the face and questioned in even greater detail. My godmother called the sheriff and advised them I had gotten lost and there was no abduction. Apparently, as I later learned, they were making contingency plans since they were perplexed how I could have just disappeared right outside the house. All I admitted to was that I was cold, confused and lost, all of which were absolutely true. At the doctor's office, I heard talking about my losing vital parts. As I gained feeling back into my feet, I heard that I would be okay. All I could hear was my mind saying over and over again, "Thank you, Holy Spirit, Jesus, and Holy Mother for watching over me." I want all to know that on my journey back, I prayed to Jesus to help me find my way home, for I was devoutly earnestly steadfastly loved and loving of God's will.

Almost twenty years later during a psychotherapy session, I was talking about my bushido training under my father's tutelage. On numerous occasions my father told me that at a certain age, determined by his father in Japan, he would need to run in bare feet in winter on snow to a mountain and back. He ran in a T shirt that had two straps at the top. The distance was apparently pre-measured and prescribed. I am not absolutely clear about the facts, but at a certain predetermined location at the mountain site there was an object which my father had to bring back. As reported by my father the run was painstaking, grueling, designed to test his courage, stamina, and perseverance. Once he embarked, there was no turning back or he would lose face and that self-condemnation was worse than death, since the value in life was training one's chi to be invincible.

He once told me about a time he was robbed and challenged by three thugs and ran away. They chased him and trapped him against a fence where he could not get away from his assailants. He warned them that he was a black belt, and that if he needed to defend himself someone could die. They laughed because he had initially run away from them. They attacked him and he defended himself. One of the three ran away, the second was hospitalized with multiple injuries, and the third had to be put on a respirator.

I asked him why, if he could do the knife disengagement technique, (I had attended judo for a number of years and knew the terminology) he didn't engage them immediately. He said he had given them his watch and wallet but they were not satisfied and that is why he ran away. He said, "My life is worth more than objects, but when I had no other recourse and I warned them repeatedly, then and only then was it necessary to defend myself." This again was another object lesson about the value of life - cautioning others that possessions are passing objects that have lesser value than one's life.

The "snow feet to the mountain" ordeal was one that young men in his province went through as part of an initiation into manhood and samarium. My father never discussed whether he made it or not. It was just assumed that all of the Tani clan would succeed; if they didn't, they would just not return and that was the way that it was, just that way and no other way.

The therapist asked me if I thought there was any correlation between this story about my father and my snow feet to the mountain and back experience. I said I saw no connection and thought that the relationship between the two had no connection.

He made no interpretation other than to ask the question was there some relationship between the two stories. While returning home I felt that I made my own trial to determine in current Western society whether I was worthy to be a Samurai candidate. I recall that when the realization came to me, I felt a rush of warmth and a sensation of elation and achievement: I had 'snow feet' in my journey into night and came back keeping the outcome of my quest secret and sacred to me. I did not question which ordeal was more arduous or difficult.

Every challenge and opportunity has its antecedents. Every opportunity offers an answer to the past and adds a chapter to life experience in the here and now. Strange how at the time what motivated me seemed a mindless experience; yet in reflection my inner sheath of power and strength was forged by the simple though complex retelling of a family practice, a folk law inculcated deep into feudalistic Japanese culture and appearing for me after World War II in the forest regions of New Jersey.

To understand a child, adolescent or adult one must understand the workings of their culture [The Genogram, McGoldrick and McGoldrick, 1997]. What was important about the therapist's intervention was not giving me the answer, but asking the question. I was able to formulate a relationship of past to present and to give myself my reward without someone else removing that golden moment of self-realization. Truly, when the client understands what's so, then and only then does the therapist summarize the realization as a confirmation. Then the client is enriched as he knows what's so, and the niche is that the client gave himself the understanding and insight.

As I see it now, my silence when beaten for not communicating the complete truth was to accept that attaining one's inner mountain peaks comes from an internal process of achieving one's inner goals and realizations.

There are more self-respectful ways to achieve such realizations and mountains of the mind. This was my way.

I too passed these practices onto my children.

In retrospect, I was not a good communicator regarding the underlining structure, mores, culture and meanings. Were I to have a chance to change the past, I would have been an easier, more compassionate task mentor and not have been so elusive and detached. A diamond is forged from the harshest forces on this planet. I am a diamond in the rough and I am only beginning to appreciate that reality.

One-Eye's Last Story

From ages eleven through thirteen I studied Japanese each Saturday at the Buddhist Church on 93rd Street in Manhattan. When I was around five, my mother became a more influential part of my parenting and I disconnected from my father and his associates. While I was able to speak Japanese fairly fluently and had achieved a moderate level of comprehension, I lost the fluency that had been integral to my father's training in later years from lack of usage and the fluency of the language.

All the children in the class were second generation Japanese born in the United States and whose parents emigrated from Japan. There were four to five classes and the study books were structured to accommodate the respective classes. Taking these classes, I felt as if I had never spoken Japanese before. Somehow, through a clear break with the use of the Japanese language, I had lost the ability to speak, read or comprehend it. The children were attentive, serious, and fastidious in their work; they all had a drive and commitment to excellence. To not know or to be uncertain was infrequent and demonstrated that someone, usually me, had not done his homework impeccably.

At the Buddhist Church the children called the caretaker "One-Eye" as he walked with a blind man's cane and had a black patch over his left eye.

During the weeks prior to the New Year, the church made a traditional food called "moche," a white, pounded dough-like substance which was eventually pressed out into circles (made into two sizes) and rectangles. The moche was customarily heated in the oven at a low temperature until it became somewhat crusty at the top, and the soft dough-like rice substance would break through the surface indicating it was ready to eat. Sugar and shoyo sauce were then mixed together and this pasty sauce was used as a coating for the moche before it was eaten. Moche is customarily eaten molten hot. One needs to keep the moche moving in your mouth as it can stick to the tender flesh of your upper palette and cause a severe burn. It is like thick Sicilian pizza dough made with pounded rice instead of flour.

I reported to the church to make the traditional moche before the Christmas holidays and was informed I would be working with One-Eye. I was introduced to him by one of the obasons [elderly women at the church]. He was in the rear of the first floor of the building kneeling next to a large electric stainless steel dough making machine which has a plunger that oscillates up and down in a continuous circular motion. It was pounding the rice into a paste. The giant plunger's movement tended to separate the rice which at this point was in a paste form, white, warm and adhesive in nature, though not excessively sticky. He kept adding the complex mixture and moving the mixture to assure an even consistency. He beckoned me to kneel on the linoleum floor. He was wedged in the corner, slumped over the dough making machine. His English was poor; however, between his Japanese, English and some sign language, I understood we would work both sides of this spreading process. The plunger made a pounding sound when it hit the bottom of the large stainless steel drum. Initially the process seemed dangerous. It was clear to me that if we were to make an uncoordinated movement someone's hand would be crushed, and we moved quickly into a synchronized movement. In time my knees and back started to ache, as I was also slumped over the steel drum like vat, yet I could not ask him or the process to stop, nor could I hesitate in my hand movement until he acknowledged some next step in the process. I hoped that would be to stop and stand erect.

The process was endless and the obason came back several times to fetch some food items from an adjacent refrigerator or to casually observe without seeming to look. The pain in my knees at some point moved to numbness and then there was only back pain with needle like sharp pain, intense pricks here and there, like floaters stabbing at random. My mind seemed to screech with an echo of silent anguish. On and on and on the process went. He was relentless, of the old school, and clearly he would not stop until the process, whatever it was, was complete.

In almost perfect unaccented English he asked, "What is your name?" "Tani" I said. "Ehhh," he responded - a very Japanese response - like an 'om' of life acknowledging the universe. "What is your father's name?" "Urashiro shiro Tani." There was a very long pause, a silence which seemed unending. At this time I was reeling back and forth and felt I would pass out at any time, as well as being fearful that my hands would crisscross his and that one of us would be seriously injured. I can still experience and feel my mind screaming, "God, please free me from this unbearable experience, this excruciating pain. I cannot bear it one more second."

One-Eye seemed almost imperceptibly to change his disposition from a rather flat affect to showing some emotional response. His body language, although restricted, was more pliant, more giving, seeming to be saying or relating on a whole different level. At this point he beckoned, stopped the machine, and pulled his hands out and I dropped gracefully to my left side. It took me some time to be able to stand and to get the circulation back into my feet, but I attempted to hurry and not show my temporary disability, pain and disorientation.

Then he said, "I knew your grandfather very well." My father had never spoken of my grandfather or why he left Japan. I learned from my mother that my father left because of a family matter, a conflict which prompted him to take appropriate action. Apparently, my Grandfather had a relationship with a geisha and this was totally unacceptable to my father's love for his mother. I remained silent because I knew if I said anything to One-Eye it might trigger some understanding that I wanted to know more or that I knew nothing. If I could reduce the amount of pain and numbness, I could learn more about my grandparents, something I could never openly question because of some dark, well-hidden secret within the 'no open questioning or disobedience' code I lived under.

At some point he said "sa" which meant we were ending this phase of the process. The pain in my back seemed to be returning. He stood up as if he had knelt for only a millisecond to pick up his cane. This was the way of the development of internal strength and stamina which for me always seemed to be out of reach and unknowable. Again, my legs went numb and I had to stand and not show discomfort or awkwardness. It felt as if I was learning how to walk all over again with a random pin-ball needle like pain that was extraordinary.

"I used to work for your grandfather; there were hundreds of us in the field," he said as he turned around and showed me a large Japanese character written in I believe catagana, the more sophisticated Japanese alphabet. "It had a large circle like this and in the center we had your family name Tani." I said "Hi," with the right inflection to acknowledge my acceptance of what he said as if saying "yes I understand," but in an adolescent's diminutive acceptance of "the word". (The use of "hi" has a multitude of inflections, all indicating a separate and very distinct acknowledgment in Japanese communication.) I thought I was lying by saying the one syllable "hi," because in fact I knew nothing of my grandparents or the Tani's. Within the Bushido Code to lie is a cardinal sin, a shameful act, a complete loss of integrity and cause for severe consequences. One-Eye continued with, "Your grandfather was a most generous man. He was the grand master in Japan, the yokozuna" (top of the sumo wrestlers' hierarchy)." "He was never defeated in his long illustrious career, but then you must know all this." This time I hesitated a long time before again responding "hi," sheepishly, almost as if I sounded like a girl. These were the only words he ever said to me from that moment on.

I couldn't get home fast enough to advise my father what happened at the Buddhist Church with One-Eye. My father seemed detached and unrelated to what I had said. He neither corroborated nor embellished the story. Now, however, it was clear to me why my father had told me stories that three to four grown men could not move one of my grandfather's legs, no matter how hard they pushed, tugged or pummeled. When I naively told this story at school, glorifying my grandfather, not only was I ridiculed but they tested my story by having only one other student move my leg with relative ease and with hardly any exertion.

The following week everyone from the Buddhist Church picked up their moche orders. Ours was probably one of the largest orders since the rectangular and circular ones were also used as displays (as if in a sanctuary or religious alter) and, as dictated by the tradition of offering moche as gifts from one family to another, my father gifted many people.

My father said, "I will go with you today to pick-up the moche." This was a strange statement because he never would accompany me. I carefully said something like I could manage bringing the order home, but he was already putting on his coat. When we were some thirty feet from the church, he reminded me of my story about One-Eye and his account of my grandfather and asked me to identify One-Eye. I repeated that it was Mr. Sato and he still wanted me to point him out. Now we were less than six feet from the basement entrance of the Church. I benevolently said it was the man with one eye as there was only one such man who was also the caretaker. Just at that moment Mr. Sato entered the room and was relatively close to the front window so I pointed him out to my father. My father gazed through the window and then asked me if I was certain that was the man and I said, "yes," completely mystified and confused. He asked me to wait outside for a few moments and then come in. It was cold and I was confused as to what meaning his questions had, what this entire conversation was about, and why he had accompanied me to the Buddhist Church. I could see him go into the church and they were acknowledging one another. He spoke privately with One-Eye for several moments and it appeared that he was whispering into Mr. Sato's ear to avoid being heard. Upon entering, I paid my respects to Mr. Sato, "do deska Kobayashison [how are you]." He stood erect, staring forward, made no customary greeting, remained silent and never ever spoke to me again.

After that encounter I realized I had betrayed his confidence and in some way damaged our relationship forever. To this day I am unaware of why my father ended any communication with Mr. Sato. Whenever I was in the room with One-Eye, he seemed to know of my presence with his scant poor vision, but he ceased all communication, even until his death some years later.

What is my lesson to be learned from this unfortunate climactic experience? The answers are many and none. At that time it seemed as if one must always be discrete, careful, withholding, not to reveal or share, to be mindful at all times everywhere that what one says has major meaning and repercussions. One must stand guard over one's understanding of the world and learn how to share insights and understandings. Maybe the truth at that time was something like such or not. I could not ask relevant revealing questions. Somehow I had to learn the truth from some inner didactic question and answer. I had to read the world by not asking, "why, how, what, when, or who?" Asking my mother was not appropriate as the code of behavior was that only when life is revealed by your father can you know what is so.

New York University "How Study" Versus "Self Study"

Straubenmueller Textile High School transitioned to become the commercial high school, Charles Evan Hughes High School in Chelsea. I transitioned too, from a commercial program to an academic program, basically in a staircase of confusion while struggling through academic hurdles.

I had joined The Japanese American Methodist Church of Christ and by my senior year had become president of the Young People's Organization which was comprised principally of second generation Japanese Americans and several second generation Chinese American students. They were all on the honor roll, attaining 100's in most if not all their Regents examinations and were destined to go to leading universities with scholarships. Neal McCaliff, the Minister, asked me to come to his residence at Columbia University's Union Theological Seminary which was an unusual request that I did not question. I saw him at least twice a week, once at our weekly Young People's meeting and a second time at Sunday service. The floors were immaculate, glazed clean and there was a serene quietude as I approached his room: I was very anxious that I had done something seriously wrong. Behind him was a very comprehensive concordance on the bible. He asked me one of the most important questions of my life:

"George, are you going to college?" I was shocked at the question and embarrassed. Why was he asking this question when I was going to a commercial school and had such great concerns about not being able to spell or write in a comprehensive manner? I attempted to explain I was not in the academic program, not at Bronx Science or Stuyvesant as my other contemporaries in the Youth Fellowship; and he responded, "I am sure if you change to an academic program you will be able to succeed." He appeared genuinely shocked that I was not going to college. As a child responding to an incredulous unrealizable quest in life, I said, "Do you really think that, Neal?"

Our meeting was brief, but he made an indelible, immeasurable contribution to my sense of who I was and what I could be. That following Monday I went to the registrar's office and changed to the academic program. I was carefully counseled about the grievous mistake I was making, reminded that I would need to take the New York State Regent exams which were very difficult, and they cautioned about my poor scholastic standing. When I said I understood, I realized that I was acknowledging the possibility that I would not be graduated from high school and that I could fail, given the complexity and demands of an academic program. In a simple fifteen minute outreach, Neal McCauliff changed the course of my destiny and empowered me to make choices I did not think were available to me.

I entered New York University's School of Commerce, Accounting and Finance in 1956 with grave misgivings. My commitment and dedication to excel were my strongest allies. My struggles with poor reading and comprehension skills, writing run on sentences, and grasping at syntax resulted in two failures during my freshman year.

Reporting to the Assistant Dean's office was a long walk to doom and gloom. Two other students were sitting in stick-like West Point body posture, waiting for harbingers of things to come. The Assistant Dean asked, "What's your name?" "Oh, yes, yes, my name is George Tani." It seemed clear he was going to address my issue in front of the two other students, only one of whom I had seen before on campus. "Mr. Tani, we need to advise you that you are being expelled from NYU because you failed two courses." The other two students quickly looked at each other and then with downcast eyes seemed to show genuine concern. "Our policy at NYU is that once a student is expelled, they are not permitted to return. Is what I am saying clear to you?"

I said, "Well, if I take six months to a year off and study English harder, I know that I will...."

"You didn't hear me; our policy is that once we expel a student under no circumstances will you be allowed to return."

This exchange went on several more times, approached from different points of view, until I clearly restated exactly what he said.

Acknowledging his communication I then responded, "I know I have a problem with English, but I will master that and it is my intention, separate from NYU's policy, to reapply in the fall."

The finality of the sound of his office door closing and the rattle of the glass window seemed to shatter my dreams of a college education. Saying what I said with two other people in the room felt humiliating, yet necessary, but how would I ever overcome my learning issues (I did not know then that I had dyslexia – I had not been assessed). I walked home feeling barren, sensing complete loss and failure with no prospect of a future. My father had said that in order for me to succeed I would need to get a college education. My interpretation was that as a Eurasian, for me to succeed I would need a miraculous intervention just to be employable.

I quickly found a job as a stock clerk at a mercantile company since the manager was my father's friend. I searched and found a book written by Johnathan Robinson entitled *How to Study* and spent what felt like months reading this oversized book over the summer. Then I outlined the sections that seemed important. The leading principles were as follows:

1. Always sit at the same desk area when you are studying.
2. Arrive at pre-determined times and arrange a pre-determined study schedule.
3. Break down the reading assignment by scanning the entire chapter first, then reading the summary, if one is available, for an overview of the subject being covered.
4. Break down the English language into those segments in which you are weak and practice building strengths in those areas.

I reapplied to New York University School of Business, Accounts and Finance and was readmitted in the Fall of 1957; it was rather perfunctory and without much consternation. I arrived at 8:30 am awaiting the opening of the main library in Greenwich Village Square at the main library. The library closed at 10:00 pm. On Sundays the library schedule was extended and opened at noon, and so I arrived in a timely fashion for that day. The librarian looked like the actor Sidney Greenstreet, with a double breasted blue suit and watch chain as well as a wind up watch. He seldom if ever indulged in any extraneous conversation. He was all about his job as a librarian. He maintained absolute silence in that library and for sure that silence helped me to concentrate.

After I returned to NYU I remember reading a chapter in management as part of an Executive Management Program, a cross-section study of business practices. The first time I finished reading the chapter I was so numb and confused I didn't even remember what subject I was reading. The second time I remembered it was management. The third time I recalled the chapter title. The fourth time I recalled some of the sub-titles. After the fifth consecutive reading I was able to recall only some of the major issues in the chapter. I then made an exhaustive list of words I didn't know, or couldn't spell, as well as noting confusing notions or concepts. I broke down the English language into spelling, grammar, syntax, word usage, vocabulary, and punctuation. I recall there were some six sections with corresponding paperback texts that provided a learning annex, plus a dictionary. Index cards were an essential part of this study program. Almost three hours had elapsed since I began reading and I had an additional chapter to read in that text and three other texts with two chapters required for each course to complete that week's reading.

I remembered my father's mentoring, "There will be times that only because you say so will you continue when in your experience all else fails you." I felt beaten, incomplete, stupid, and totally overwhelmed. No one could ever master such an avalanche of learning requirements. On one list alone, the one with the words I couldn't spell, I had 67 words. I remember that number since it was one more number than my street address. The words I didn't know were not quite as numerous but closely approximated that number.

In the weeks and months that comprised the following four years, I had few friends, but my pursuit was constant and faithful. Hour after hour, day after day, my commitment was unfaltering. Months and then years elapsed dedicated to study, study, study.

For me to complete my studies the available library time was insufficient and so I needed to search out other study facilities. Eventually I discovered the Law Library stacks which remained open until either 1:00 or 2:00 am. Reading on the subway, returning home at 2:30 am and leaving again at 8:00 am (so as not to be late for my designated study chair) made the challenge long and arduous.

Other than church on Sunday, Chock Full of Nuts lunch or dinner breaks, classes, and occasional bathroom breaks, my vigil continued until I graduated in January, 1969, with a B.S. degree, taking six courses in my final semester at NYU and earning an A in all but one course. Students in the liberal arts library believed I was either a pre-med student or writing my dissertation. I completed my B.S. degree in four and one-half years.

The Long Beach Island Swim to Open Seas, *Ocha Deska, Snow Feet to the Mountain and Back*, and other training exercises my father had inspired all facilitated my sense of commitment in achieving my goals to read and write and complete college.

Post World War II anti-Japanese sentiment, my Asian appearance, and my own solitary confinement forced me to limit my socialization and my ability to relate to others. My own negative self image and perception of the world around me hindered me from getting help from the university and others. There was substantial shame in not being able to read and write and I found it impossible to reveal this to others. Also, the Japanese way is to be self-reliant and compliant. Other Japanese families were very much committed to their children succeeding and were able to provide supportive interventions even if English was not their first language. My parents lived separate lives, were never expressive in public, did not believe in being seen together in public, lived in two different zones in the same apartment, and had no common friends. Perhaps they inculcated in me a belief system of separatism and a deep division in common objectives.

Both my parents were illiterate in English but had proficiency in their own languages.

When I went to Columbia University's learning disability center, the teacher asked me how long I had known that I was dyslexic. I was 26 years old and had no clue. When I was in my early or late forties, a friend said they experienced my mother as being dyslexic and began to cite several key traits which had no reality in my experience: she was just my mother. Some of those traits she observed were her hand writing, never leaning to write English and her reporting she was a very slow learner in grade school in Hungary may have been some indication of some of the characteristics of being dyslexic.

I remember another code of conduct I learned from my father regarding the need for a Samurai's strength and stamina. A Samurai must always know his limits. My father always said, "When drinking Sake only drink until one more sip might leave you defenseless." One must always be ready to battle the forces of life. To be slovenly in one's practice is not only to lose face, it is to be defenseless in one's commitment to family and the noble truths of Buddhism. (My father practiced the Shinto faith and attended services with some regularity at the Buddhist church in New York City.) Substantially into my third year a Philippine master's degree student's insistence prompted me to go to the student lounge at Loeb Student center at NYU. He was amazed at my study routine and asked if I ever dated or took breaks. I reported, "Very few." He encouraged me to take time to have fun and pointed out that dating was also a part of life and not to be minimized. He paid for my coffee and sandwich. I went with him with great reluctance. At some point he asked me to look around and tell him what I saw. Perhaps for the first time I saw what appeared to be hundreds of people laughing, talking, relaxing and sharing common experiences. My last glance was at a couple who were standing some twenty feet away, laughing and having fun as two girls joined them, such a simple scene and so powerfully illuminating. When the student is ready the teacher will arrive.

When he left I cried, for I knew he was a messenger of truth, compassion, life and living. I knew he loved me and wanted me to grow. From that moment on I made more time for personal, private time, leisure time, dating and really enjoyed being open to people and their experiences. It wasn't too long after that that I met my first wife and we were married in 1970. She made an incredible contribution to my life not only academically, but also in her sharing her love and sensitivity with me. She graduated magna cum latte from NYU undergraduate school and had a full scholarship in philosophy.

The Magical Dwarf at New York University

While attending New York University I experienced an event that helped me focus and to learn more about telepathy, psychometrics, clairvoyance, having visions and being a mystic. I was unemployed and had heard of the New York University Employment Center postings. Once there, I filled out an application and was advised to return later in the day for an interview with a female counselor. I arrived about ten minutes late and it appeared that everyone in the office had left, but the door was open so I went in. It seemed strange that the lighting had been substantially reduced and that there was no receptionist as there had been earlier in that day. I may be mistaken, but I believe there was a cleaning person who appeared in the office at some point during this experience. I walked to the back of the office area and called the name of the person I was supposed to see. No one immediately responded, but shortly thereafter a woman who appeared to be a dwarf said, "Are you Mr. Tani?" I said, "Yes. " She replied, "Please follow me. You're late and I didn't think you were coming." I made two right turns and went into her office. I was dressed in a blue pin striped suit from Brooks Brothers, a chesterfield coat, black wing-tipped shoes and other executive accoutrements. She said, "Please tell me about you." I started to describe my degrees and past work history and was well into a walk-through résumé review when she said, "You know this is not what we were meant to speak about." I said, "What should we be speaking about?" and she replied, "You are on a journey and I believe I can be of assistance to you." My recollection of our conversation was that she told me something about my father, why I entered this world, and, was probably clear in her understanding but cryptic to me, about my life mission.

Somehow, she knew something about my spirituality and my connections with being a psychic and that my mother was a prominent psychic in New York City, reading tarot cards. After a short period of time, I became very concerned about the dwarf lady. I felt that something ominous and dangerous was about to happen or was happening and I actually doubted my reality. She reassured me and accelerated our conversation by saying several important things, namely, that when I went to the book store, up the street, I should place my hand over the front of bookcases, and when my hand became warm that was where some book was that I needed to read. She also spoke of the red room and something in a recommended reference book that was very important for me to know. Curiously, while I found and purchased the book [title unrecalled], I never located the red room or the important information from the reference book.

I was escorted out to the front of the office and perhaps less than one hour had elapsed. I did notice it was dark outside, but then it was late into the spring. I returned the next day and asked to speak again to the lady I had seen the prior night, as much of what she had said was unclear and mysterious. They said that no one of that description worked there and that at that time the office was closed and no one could gain entry. When I became somewhat more demanding about what had occurred I noted that an NYU security guard who was near the front of the building was noticing or at least it appeared he was noticing my agitated behavior, and perhaps was about to enter the office and it seemed best to conclude my quest for the dwarf lady. Probably the NYU security guard had coincidentally located himself near the front door as their general office was several doors down; however, the strangeness of this incident, the first of its kind, made me very edgy. I recognize this kind of thinking is paranoid in nature and the incident could be described as delusional and or hallucinatory. However, about a week later, I saw this same women walking across the street on Washington Place South, but when I rushed up the block to my right, the same block in which the Placement Center was located, she was nowhere to be found; she had disappeared. Since she was a dwarf, there was no way she could have out-distanced my dash of less than 100 feet. My question was how she could just disappear like that? I know what I know and it did happen. I am clearly not in the habit of seeing things that are not there. I have never seen this woman again, nor anyone that even looked remotely like her. What was important about this experience was that I purchased some ten to fifteen books from that local store and began a journey of learning about the occult, wizardry, witchcraft, psychics, mediums, out of body experiences and other subjects in the psychic realm.

I would arrive at Bobst Library early in the morning in 1984 and read until late at night, and my wife Rosalyn was most accommodating while working on my masters in social work. Because of my learning disorder, I found it very difficult to concentrate if there was any noise or disturbance in my immediate environment. On the eighth or ninth floor at Bobst Library, other than a few casual conversations which seemed to end as quickly as they began, the quiet was a constant. When I became tired of reading, I walked the quadrangle just outside the library doors on the ninth floor. I would regain my momentum; tiredness would seem to melt away and book after book would be absorbed. I cannot say that I am a student who recalls or remembers titles of books or authors, nor can I recall technical data or repeat the processes that the texts seemed to highlight. That did not seem to matter. Perhaps in some way this is part of my dyslexia. I read book after book, some selected by the heat that was generated as I passed my hand over the shelves at the up the street bookstore.

The Convergence

The early 1980's represented a convergence of creative imaginary, miraculous opportunities and visions in the formation of multiple companies, developing breakthrough processes, psychic readings, healings and refining the ability to channel and listen to guided messages; not to leave out being designated a Messenger of God.

The seminal moment or causative condition that gave rise to these innate growth experiences seem to be on the one hand a strong relationship to God and on the other hand to be in search of the miraculous as a contribution to others. It is true that what you ask for can be created in the space of miracles especially if the igniting forces represent the journey of the Gypsy Samurai.

In the early 1980's the creative communication employment supported my work as a Support Intensive Leader to contribute focus and outcomes for executives in the area of work, relationship and family, health and spirituality. Earning a two-year certificate in natural and spiritual healing techniques at the Center in Massachusetts strengthened my knowledge of herbs, nutrition, massage, foot reflexology, spiritual development and most importantly these areas of study were directly related to body systems and diseases and corresponding remedies graduating on August 25, 1983. Journey over and beyond earned its charter of incorporation on August 8, 1980. Its contribution to my search for making a difference in people's lives was to "identify solutions of problems of others or to an improvement in their functioning." Breakthrough Experience was incorporated on October 16, 1980 and its primary purpose was to formulate trainings of groups of 15 people over a five to six month period to breakthrough blocks and barriers using state of the art technology such as video playback, face mask therapy, comprehensive biopsychosocials, and some 77 processes were trademarked and integrated into a training called Breakthrough Experience. At the end of this period of time which was June 1984 I entered New York University School of Social work and graduated in 1986 moving into a clinical social work position at Albert Einstein College of Medicine.

Creative Communication Corporation

―――――――――――――――― ❧ ――――――――――――――――

While an executive trainer in the early 1980's, conducting Support Intensives for fifteen people, I experienced extraordinary breakthroughs in working with people. One of the primary purposes of the workshop was to facilitate executives to breakthrough blocks or barriers in such areas as relationship, career, health and vitality as well as other goal oriented areas.

The initial group session dealt with scheduling. The first session was probably one of the most challenging sessions in the sequence, since these executives were customarily out of town or had pressing commitments and there had to be a consensus of dates chosen as everyone needed to attend the fifteen scheduled sessions. It was inevitable that many of the executives had to adjust their schedules to accommodate a group that would meet three times a month.

Participants would have a designated evening in which they would present their lives and their goals. Customarily their immediate family was present, as well as their significant others and close friends. Prior to their evening, I would have an initial clearing session with an individual, develop an agenda and support them to be focused on their desired outcomes. First, I would determine underlying blocks and barriers to their achieving their stated objectives. Then we would work to formulate a list of the services or support systems they needed to achieve those objectives which they could request from the powerful executives that were enrolled in their Support Intensive. My role was that of facilitator.

I apprenticed for the first group, being trained by 'HS' who was an amazing coach and guru. As my groups coalesced and became more and more contributory as family to one another, something rather extraordinary occurred during our tri monthly meetings; there were amazing breakthroughs transforming people's lives.

Customarily two people would be talking. I would at some point place my hands on the respective backs of these two people who were working through some perhaps long-standing unresolved issue or desired outcome. People in the group would say, "Did you see that? It's incredible."

The groups grew larger and larger with family and friends until we had to set a limit on the number of people attending; the word was out that extraordinary happenings were common-place each week.

A member of the group who was a sports medicine doctor was working through some issues with his mother. When his mother sent him to the United States from the West Indies, he felt she had abandoned him and he could not resolve those feelings of loss, separation from his family and growing up in a new culture with different traditions and beliefs. Her actions marked and excoriated his life with regard to trust and women. Clearly, he had an excellent marriage and children that he loved and contributed too; nevertheless, this life event dampened his, what should we call it, self love, nurturing, and trust, sense of being loved and other siblings were not transported elsewhere and remained at home to be nurtured by his mother and that family constellation which was extensive.

At some point my hands were raised up again resting gently on the upper backs of both son and mother, very close to their heart charkas. They slowly engaged in more detailed conversations and his mother spoke of needing to take the action of removing her son to give him greater opportunities and of loving him dearly, perhaps even more than her other children. Her son began to cautiously question her actions, recalling incidents and moments of separation. Gradually, her sacrifice and her actions became clear as a proud woman explained her dilemma. He began to internalize the magnitude of his mother's actions, her sacrifice, the hard decisions she had to make, thinking about him and not herself. A solitary tear or two descended his face and for those that knew him, many understood this was no easy access point; he had crossed over, understood the circumstances and forgiven his mother.

A lifetime of anger, resentment and feelings of abandonment can be assuaged in a moment when a catharsis occurs: we can all let go of our justifications and excuses, some held for a lifetime, when we engage the truth and begin to accept what is so. She was a large, seriously penetratingly take-charge woman, her face smooth but severely drawn as if by iron braces into a stern alabaster facial tonality. She held her son as if not even a fifth dimension force could dislocate him; God help the man who would remove her son at that moment, for his soul would perish as a protective mother poured a lifetime of love into his drained memory banks. They were at one with the other, and it had taken a lifetime to embrace their oneness in channeling the energy of vision and forgiveness. The room became silent with the love and power of this mother and son, who had finally understood the sacrifices parents make and that those sacrifices are not without pain and suffering.

Quite often even when we say what is in our hearts, we are not understood. Time can heal all wounds but eventually we need to make time to freshen up our actions to give them more meaning in time, repeating the why and how of our actions, never assuming another understands the underlying reasons for our actions or the thoughts giving rise to those actions.

Be crystal clear in your communication when you change directions in life, for if you leave even a small partial uncertainty, the message you leave can have the opposite impact or outcome than you anticipated.

In another incident in the same workshop a husband, had difficulty communicating with his wife. His father's relationship to his mother clouded his ability to be more fully expressed and clear in his communication with his own wife. His wife's interpretation of her husband's intentions and behavior was that they were undeclared, confused and lacking any commitment to take concerted action. At a critical juncture during his evening he was asked to put on a dress which was available in the apartment where we held the Support Intensive. While his stalwart VMI backbone told him to resist putting on feminine clothes, his courage and willingness to trust the process persuaded him to accede to the request; and gradually he worked through his trapped feelings of a strong, coercive mother and retiring father who had been relegated to the basement of his own home. Once again the room filled with tears as each and every person saw some part of themselves coming to term with our interjects [the internalized parental values and behaviors we assimilate] and the need to better understand our past to live more meaningfully lives. At the end of the process, with tears and rejoicing in her face his wife stood up and said, "I love you. I will always and forever love you. I always have known who you are, and I know now you have found a place to understand and not live downstairs as your father did. You can be self declared and powerful. That's who you are." When they hugged, everyone in the room, one by one, stood up and one hand joined another and there was silent bonding and acknowledgment as the group coalesced; people were whole and complete, with no one and nothing left out.

This was the nature of the work; what was created for the person working in this group dynamic, as well as their respective counterpart be it a parent, marital partner or significant other or life event, was the stage of development and history that set a mal-adaptive behavior in place. Recreate the experience with guidance and wisdom and channeling from a higher power and what arrives is a moment in time when the past can be forgiven in the present, right here and right now.

Being an open channel and guided by a commitment to make breakthroughs for people and as well the will of Mother Divine and the forces of the truth to be free from restraints causes a new perspective and integration of what can be, what should be and what will be. The courage and will of human beings is to search for and find the miraculous and not to be trapped or controlled by restraining forces so often cradled by past events. God is Good and God is Great and his domain comes to those committed to make a difference in the lives of other people; I am committed to the well-being of others and this domain opens spaces and places which are life altering for me and for others.

God was in our midst. As people felt called upon internally to share and contribute to a larger body of experience for this husband to draw from and the individual sharing to benefit from, each participant's statement gave rise to wisdom and knowing what and why and who and when and how we could let go of our past and accept what powerful beings we can be each day of our lives. My hands were once again extended on both the husband and wife's backs, touching their heart charkas. Where you might ask does that healing embracing energy come from; perhaps the answer is one's self directed calling to make a difference and as well calling for God's grace and blessing as a messenger of empowerment and transmutation.

A number of years later I spoke to the two ministers who lead the Center of the Light Trainings, having attended their first two year program to become a Healing Practitioner in September 1982. I asked one of them, since we were talking about transmitting energy and faith healing, if this could be done with one's hands not on both sides of an impacted body part such as an arm, leg or chest area, but with hands resting outside the perimeter of two people, by placing one hand on the backs of two people facing one another. Eva said she had not heard of anyone being able to do this, and requested that I explain what experiences occurred after one's hands were placed in this way. After I related several Support Intensive experiences, she said that it very much appeared as if my energy was able to affect people breaking through to realizations and discoveries. Most importantly, she said that the work that was being done appeared to have some lasting effect. She also said that I had extraordinary intuitive abilities and was able to language breakthroughs that combined with the transmission of healing energies. There and then I had some greater understanding of how God was channeling his love, insight and forgiveness through me as a healing channel. "Thank you, God, for allowing me to make a difference."

The Journey Over and Beyond

When I was 42 as I ended my career in the corporate world, I created an organization on October 20, 1980: Journey Over and Beyond.

The key phrase in Journey's Certificate of Incorporation is "all as required or expedient to a solution of problems of others or to an improvement in function."

Upon awakening one morning, I thought: "I could facilitate the elimination of any physical or mental health condition during a one-on-one experience lasting approximately 4 ½ hours." This realization resulted from a dream about what comprises this experience.

The 'voice' in the dream said: "Use the black board, dyadic processes, hypnosis, psychic channeling, shamanic journaling, serve lunch and most important, work with individuals who would "name and disclose what unacceptable condition of their life they wanted to resolve or change."

Several months later, I created Breakthrough Experience, Inc. (BE), principally a management consulting businesses for companies with annual revenue of 5 million or less. BE consisted of a fifteen session workshop for executives of these organizations. I facilitated this workshop from December, 1980 through1984, stopping several months before entering New York University School of Social Work.

BE workshops lasted five to six months and there were a minimum of three sessions each month. The intent of this workshop: participants to relinquish an undesired and unwanted behavior and/or manifest a defined objective. The workshops had a specific learning segment, including working through issues that collectively tend to keep people stuck in unproductive patterns and beliefs. Testimonials from some of the participants are provided below to illustrate some of their accomplishments:

President of a communications organization:

"What I learned from this program is that most of the surface issues you and I are used to dealing with have hidden roots which lead deep into your past. Without being fully aware of why certain fears exist or certain self-defeating behavioral patterns develops, you may never truly experience your full potential."

Executive Director of Higher Education"

"The only things that anyone can get out of BBO are **results!** There is no choice in that. Frequently, the results are the ones you think you want. That makes BBO sometimes comfortable.

Vice President for Advertising:

"I want to thank you for supporting me to finally take a stand on myself"

Data Services Company President

"Breakthrough by Objective has meaningfully and significantly moved my existing Management by Objective program by putting people in touch with their personal blocks and barriers."

President, advertising agency

"Directly from this seminar I have been better able to deal more directly in business with amazing results. This not only has had a positive effect on my work, but with those I interact with."

Attorney

"Among many other benefits, I found BBO helped me to identify goals and objectives, analyze the methods by which I habitually went about achieving {or not achieving] them and then systematically created processes and structures for expanding my own methodologies. In particular, I found the videotaping sessions extremely revealing and beneficial."

The outline below represents the training program that facilitated the program. There were some 77 or so dyadic and group processes that were trademarked and customarily seventeen to twenty-two of these processes were selectively utilized in BE on a weekly basis; each process had a measured outcome and relationship to that weeks training. As the program developed Dolly Saroka made face masks for the participants which enabled everyone to be their anonymous safe secure self in portraying themselves in an exercise. Also, the use of video equipment allowed participants to see themselves and to capture moments of truth and working through difficult issues, the instant replay of critical scenes again facilitated deepening the members understanding of underlining issues, reactions, stuck points, self realizations and participants could take the video home and benefit from breakthrough moments and experiences. Seeing is believing; believing is seeing and putting into action the missing parts of moving from expectations to being the expectation.

The Howard Johnson Story

———⚮———

In the 1980's I was always late for appointments. While I was on the Board of Directors of New York City program, and I was rushing to the Howard Johnson Restaurant on 42nd street for an 8:00 A.M. meeting. When I arrived the meeting had already convened and the President, was engaged in leading a discussion.

I found a seat in a long column of men and women facing one another; there were at least fifteen of us. As I became engaged in the subject and well into the course of the varied issues being presented, my hand became warm and I felt the flow of healing energy and I noticed that my right arm and hand was parallel to 's right shoulder. My inner voice said Bill was having a heart attack. While I knew him casually, my internal conversation was that he was too young, virile, and active to be having a heart attack. I thought that what I could do without disturbing him was to contribute a silent healing. I positioned the palm of my hand downward as we were sitting in a booth and began praying for his health and well-being by drawing the pain off in an imaginary visualization. I began to perspire. Once or twice he looked over at me and we engaged in a smile or perhaps reflective acknowledgement. I continued to focus my concentration on the perceived yet imaginary pain in his chest. While at the Center of the Light, we were taught how to go into our space and meditate, draw pain off through focused concentration and then in intermittent movements flick one's hand or hands several times to throw off the negative energy. The meeting ended and Bill turned to me and said, "You can't believe what happened to me just a short while ago. I thought that I was having a heart attack, and there was this pain in my chest right here." "Really, when did it happen"? "Well, I guess, maybe ten or fifteen minutes ago." I remained silent about the information my inner voice provided.

Therapeutic touch is a healing technique developed by Dolores Kreager, RN., and practiced for a period of time at New York University, by bringing healing energy to her patient by sensing areas on the body where heat was emanating from the etheric surface of the skin. During this healing technique the body of the client is never touched.

I said to Bill, "Sounds like you should see a doctor, just to rule out your concerns." "For sure, for sure, I'm scheduling an appointment today." I had learned that oftentimes it is best to remain removed from gaining noticeable attention and taking any credit; people need to take actions that best fit their sense of what's appropriate to remedy their health concerns.

He went on to say that he noticed, sometime after I sat down, an incredible amount of heat emanating from his right shoulder. This healing experience was somewhat different from that of others since at some point I lost my awareness of the healing process and shifted into an altered state concentrating on his health and well being. Some aspect of my being was listening to the discussion, some part was engaged in healing his heart, and some part was becoming at one with pulling off the pain and channeling that energy upward toward the ceiling and away from us (corresponding to the process I had learned at the Center of the Light).

Sometimes a person may desire to say something, perhaps to take credit or to speak of their "specialness" but that would have been completely inappropriate. In the movie <u>Resurrection</u>, the character played by Ellen Burstyn performs several healings, and throughout that movie I cried as I closely related to her gifts of the spirit and her work. The character she played made a difference and asked for no credit; she oftentimes wished to remain anonymous and in doing so there was a minimization of ego and selfdom. In this space of anonymous existence we remain in Gods ordinance of wisdom, love, contribution empowerment of his will not ours. Over the years this has been one of the learning lessons for me.

What realm of consciousness does a human being enter to generate a belief system that can receive information and bring about some form of healing just by being close to another being? Perhaps, only perhaps, the essence of such healing comes from becoming an advocate for such work and maintaining a diligence in a non-ending search to focus one's commitment to being a healing channel. So often, more in the past than in the present, most assuredly among transformed people, and in certain healing centers, the power of one's awareness is greater because of one's being in tune with the frequency and open to the listening. When one is committed to causes a whole series of realities occur that would never have been possible were the individual not so focused.

The channel of love has countless frequencies; our desire to attune opens ways and means to serve. Selflessness keeps us focused on the outcome of health and wellness, not our personal aggrandizement, but an I Am reality; yes I am me but also I choose to use my being in the service of others without a base line of anticipated credit, selfdom, notoriety or personal gratification or me-ness: in this sacred space lives one's nature to receive the bonding silent message of someone near you to make a contribution too.

The FW W Story

There came a time when the process of healing, clairvoyance and penetrating the veil of miracles was emerging. During these years I created a process called the Breakthrough Experience (trademarked & incorporated.) As part of this process I claimed that I could facilitate the elimination of any physical or mental condition that was perceived as an affliction, if the client was willing to have it disappear.

As I recall Faith was one of my very first clients in 1983. I had not seen Faith for some time, and true to her fastidious nature she was precisely on time. I rang her in and to my amazement when she approached the door; she appeared as someone I did not know. "George," she said. The first thought I had was that this woman was not Faith, yet she came at the very same moment in time that I expected Faith. I didn't even hear her say my name; clearly I was confused and perplexed. We both stared at one another for a moment and then she said, "What's the matter George, don't you recognize me?" Upon hearing her last word I gathered my senses and Faith appeared as if by some metamorphosis. She was more than perplexed; she was disturbed and bordering on being angry. She looked tired, older than I remembered her, and she was mildly contorted in her physical stance. I was embarrassed and confused. What had happened to Faith that she had so physically changed? "Were you expecting me? You seemed to not even recognize me." I quickly responded, "Oh no, I was just preoccupied, that's all." For sure I did not want to dramatize how my confusion might in some way reflect on her almost complete alteration in appearance. Immediately, as she sat down, I realized that my best friend, Joe, had sent his mother to be healed physically and not to remove some emotional block or barrier. At that moment I felt a sense of moderate fear and uncertainty, for I knew that her afflictions were many and that perhaps this healing required greater ability than I thought I had.

I experienced a moment of despair or confusion regarding exactly what this Breakthrough Experience represented. Until this moment I never even mildly challenged my ability to cause change. Joe had sent a test for me; yet clearly it was what I said I could do. I realized that God was setting the challenge early in the process of my work. I earnestly indicated to Faith that my primary concentration was focused on behavioral change and not on physical change. I felt somewhat humbled by this experience and at the same time felt as if my claim was truly a fantasy, for no one in my experience could create nor claim such an ability to remove physical infirmity, whatever their ailment was revealed to be. Faith responded that her son said I could do the impossible, the miraculous. I said, "I will work on the mental blocks and barriers and at the end of our session I will work on the physical."

I attempted to appear confident and gave assurances, but my faith in my abilities was clearly shaken by my own beliefs of what is possible and improbable. I also felt that if I did not produce a result so that she was satisfied, I would not take my fee for the session.

"I guess you know why I am holding my head like this." I responded "No." "Well I thought you knew what people were thinking." The internal dialogue began again; here she was challenging my core beliefs. How was it that I did not know why she was holding her head that way? She went on to say that if she let her head go and did not hold her chin, her head would move to the right or my left. I believe that I did recognize that her sciatica was causing her great discomfort and pain at different times during our session together.

"I need to be honest Faith. There are many things that I do not know, but I will work to the best of my ability to bring about a Breakthrough Experience. If you in anyway are not satisfied, then please do not pay me." I said this without affect or innuendo. She responded, "I know you will do your best, and that is all I really expect."

We covered her issues by my recording a mind map, a very comprehensive psychosocial history, encompassing her family system, developmental conflicts, crises, interpersonal relationships and a myriad of other significant milestones. At the time Faith was 69. As I recall we needed two sheets of an oversized artist sketch pad to record her life history. After almost two hours, we started the next stages of the process: a body relaxation process; an alignment process; an eyes-closed client question period; and my psychic interpretations. Faith life had been an arduous history of trials and tribulations; although there seemed to be a few respites from hardships and overcoming life's challenges.

At the end of this stage of the experience we took a break for lunch. FW said little about the benefits or accuracy of my interpretations or summary observations. I felt somewhat uncomfortable getting no feedback, yet felt it was inappropriate to question her about her experience, unless she wished to comment about it voluntarily. Infringing upon her experience would have been intrusive and thwarting, which would be counter-transferential. Lunch was prepared in advance, with minor additions such as heating the water for tea. Strangely, remembering back, I do not recall if she continued to hold her head or whether the sciatic discomfort had diminished to any extent.

I had learned therapeutic touch and through extensive readings and practice. I began the healing phase of the session. I recall feeling somewhat uncomfortable performing the therapeutic touch. Faith lay on a sumptuous couch. The eyes closed process continued. I sought out 'hot areas' and was guided by personal navigational sensitivity which seemed to last a considerable length of time. At times my mind would temporarily wander. "Was I taking too long? Since I knew this person from the past, would that make a difference? Since her physical conditions appeared severe, could my belief in my higher power of healing really make a difference?" For sure, this was the greatest challenge. Overall, my doubts were mild; nevertheless, the single central question was "Am I deluding myself with this Breakthrough Experience process?"

Faith was now sitting completely upright and said she felt better and at another time she said she felt good. She took her checkbook out and began to write her check. While she was preparing her check, my one consuming thought was had I really brought about a breakthrough experience - was she cured - was she even better? Would whatever physical changes that occurred be of a lasting nature or only transitory? Change is one of accepting the original forces that set the pattern for a particular behavior as well as physical causative factors on the physical plane. Faith said the sciatic pain had subsided. We briefly acknowledged each other at the door and as timely as she appeared, she was gone.

This process challenged my sense of value and while I felt a sense of equanimity and aliveness, the questions lingered. Had I produced the result or was this Breakthrough Experience a lot of bullshit, a sham, a hoax, not believable? Again, I experienced a lingering pang of fear. With God's intervention as the source of my healing power, a channeling of energy in his name, I doubted the powers to alter the physical just because I was acting as a conduit of healing in his name. During those early stages of the BE, my thoughts were intermingled with a sense of my own power separate from God's role and interventions in the process.

My wife and I had received tickets for Carnegie Hall from an impresario of the Soviet Émigré Orchestra. Before the show I took a brief breath of fresh air and many of my friends were inside waiting for the performance to start. I was close to the main doors and there were people waiting for companions as well as others smoking before the performance. A woman pranced up to me and gently bumped into me. She said something and I realized this was a woman who was probably disturbed. Wherever I moved, she moved as well. She seemed to want something and it was not clear what her needs involved. I felt unnerved and darted away toward the door to return to my orchestra seats by my wife. When I realized she would not stop, I became concerned and while still observing her in this brief interlude moved quickly back into Carnegie. She then quickly approached me and said, "I'm Faith, don't you recognize me? See, I don't have to hold my head any longer and my sciatic condition has completely disappeared. What you do works, George." As before, I realized instantaneously that this was Faith, Faith. She looked twenty years younger, agile, flirting around as if she was pirouetting, doing a dance of vitality with life springing forth in her limbs. We embraced and I felt at one with FW; she had been healed and was whole and complete within herself. I rejoiced, elated and revivified in my faith in my work and the power of Jesus Christ of Nazareth to revive the spirit of life and give light to her impacted limb and torso.

During the Émigré's performance I soared and tears came to my eyes as I realized that I had made a contribution and that the work I was embarking on truly had both physical and psychical contributions. I saw my friend introduce his orchestra and felt another surge as I recalled the work we had done together.

Wherever I went during those stages of seeking interpretations and tying together history and behavioral responses, inner archaic memories and meanings buried in the body and mind were translated and empowered for the being to find truth, revelations and a cathartic release of forgiveness to breakthrough. Praise God for the power to breakthrough with life's forces, for healing and generating self-realizations.

The Unknown Restaurant: Where is it

In retrospect, always creating challenges may have been an outgrowth of my desire to become a Samurai, to be at one with that special mysterious and mythical universe and face all adversity as a to-be-expected, normal, here-and-now, self-imposed reality. When feudal Japan entered the age of the firearms, the short and long sword became symbolic but futile, just as dueling in the South to avenge an insult became an anachronism. In retrospect, then, my behavior was uncommon and sometimes mal-adaptive. My earlier impetuous behavior has reconfigured itself. For me, the art of creation now lives inside of extraordinary readings, healings and contributions to those who are disadvantaged.

I had been to a wonderful Italian restaurant in Queens, N.Y. with a co-worker where I once worked from 1970 to 1975, and I had this compelling need to return there again. Taking none of the customary actions of getting the name of the restaurant, its location, or even the phone number, I went on a mission. The quest started at my parent's home on with my two children,

Peter and Nicole, and my first wife, Johanna. The self imposed challenge was to find three different vehicles selected at random off the street, and to tell the respective drivers that I needed to get to a restaurant in Queens by a designated time. I presented the requests as if an emergency was in progress. I did not offer to pay the respective drivers. Once again, I did not know the name of the restaurant, the street location nor the specific area in Queens where the restaurant was located. Johanna, as was her way, was accommodating, indeed, generous in her willingness to participate; she was a sanctioning partner on my journey.

There were four of us and from one car after another, without even a small gratuity, merely a thank you, we miraculously emerged in Queens. It was cumbersome explaining the whereabouts of the restaurant with no exact address, but I did recall that the restaurant had no menu, white tablecloths, long lines, and possibly, just possibly, a probable fragment of the name. There might have been some more tangible facts, but I believe my representation was close to, "That's it, folks." The third car, as God is my witness, dropped my family in front of the restaurant. There was a line and I created some reason why we should not have to wait to be called from a list. Perhaps they allowed us to jump the list because the children looked tired, though it was a Friday night and there was no school the next day, or perhaps they looked forlorn and were simply thinking, "Yup, another extraordinary adventure with Dad."

Our meal was wonderful. We ordered lobster, shrimp scampi and other delectable without seeing a menu. We returned home by cab and the children, in normal ride-home mode, were beginning to doze off in our arms.

As with the "Snow Feet" experience, I cannot explain why such strange behavior descended upon me or why I subjected my family to such experiences. Perhaps it's a need for domination, proving I'm Samurai, or some programmed Japanese strategy that Japanese fathers inculcate into their children and their children in turn replicate, like timed action droplets that descend in time and space leaving the outcome to the progeny. Fortunately, such episodes were relatively infrequent for my family.

Meg's Reporting of Her Journey to Medjagorie

Meg came for supportive interactive Psychotherapy at a time I was seeing clients in private practice. In one of our early sessions, at the opening of our session she reported that she was probably being considered for a position as an American speaking tour guide in Medjagorie in Yugoslavia. She went on to say that this was a good idea of mine of which I recall having no such subject conversation during any of our prior sessions. In our next week's session she reported that she not only was hired for the position, but they were going to maintain her apartment as she requested and pay her rent as part of her salary package which she again said was a good idea of mine which as well I could not recall any such conversation.. I must admit the exact issues of her reported acknowledgement are unclear; nevertheless, she did report that ideas that emanated from our prior sessions caused her to take specific actions which ultimately led Meg to go to Medjagorie.

She mentioned that 12 children had seen the Blessed mother and they were now adults and many Christians made pilgrimages to this holy site and she was drawn to be part of this religious experience. This in turn led to my next extraordinary experience when Meg sent me some eight or nine blessed pictures of the Holy Mother. The Croatian priest blessed the pictures of Mary and she as well brought those blessed pictures to the top of the mountain at Medjagorie where the Croatians had erected a cross during the Second World War in which she prayed upon the pictures of the Holy Mother for an additional blessing and mailed those colored pictures to me to contribute to whatever empowerment healing was appropriate. I still have one of those sacred pictures on my mantel. This in turn led to the next extraordinary miraculous experience.

The Atlantic Beach Hotel and Cabanna Club

I was nineteen and working my way through college as a waiter at an Atlantic Beach Hotel in New York. I had in 1957 researched the best shoes to wear as I understood waiting on tables was arduous work standing for long hours on one's feet. The black shoes had a triangular cleat like sole which were reported to be helpful in maintaining one's energy. Also, I wore black pants that had no cuffs which was trendy but not in keeping with proper dress code. I did not know that a cumber bun was an essential part of proper dress in a celebrated 5 star hotel with entertainers like Buddy Hacket and leading singers of the time. Wearing a wash and wear short sleeve shirt was clearly noticeable and the composition of my appearance and newness to waitering resulted in being fired. What I subsequently learned was that I had provided poor service to a very important member of the hotels ownership family. Reporting for my final check I waited to speak to the Manager who was encased in a glass paneled office.

Two very attractive women were sitting across from one another outside the manager's office talking about a family member who was having some issues in adaptation. They invited me to sit down as I had been standing respectfully for some time. At some point I asked if I could contribute some ideas concerning their concerns with that family member and was directly invited into the conversation. One of the two women asked if I was working on my PhD and I indicated that I was going into my sophomore year in college that September. They appeared to be amazed at my insight and contribution and asked why I was waiting. I explained I was being let go because of poor service to a member of the ownership family. At this time Cecilia asked if she could help me and speak to someone on my behalf. I replied that since I had provided poor service it would not be appropriate for anyone to intercede for me. She asked that if I did not work that summer could I afford college in the fall semester and I said probably not. There was substantial confusion about why I was being so stoic about not being helped. The women continued speaking to one another and I recall feeling very uncomfortable experiencing their willingness to help me and being fired. Cecilia at some point stood up. went to the class petitioned room and walked right into the Manager's office. She leaned over his desk and whatever she said he took one glance at me and she exited the room. All I can remember is that I sat there an interminable time waiting for my check and the discomfort was enormous; I no longer felt part of their conversation and as was being feeling disconnected and unwanted. At some point in time the most gorgeous Filipino man approached me wearing what appeared to be a tuxedo; he was the maitre d'hôtel of the dining room. He said, "Are you George Tani?", to which I responded, "Yes". He said, "We have made arrangements for you to take on room service in the morning for people who call in and as well you can be a waiter at the Majorka Room. I accepted gratefully and said I have no car to get to the Majorka Room, and he said the transportation had already been arranged. I worked room service early every morning and the Majorka Room, a private club, every night. I swam during the day to maintain energy as there was virtually minimal time to sleep as I returned home late from the club. On the 30th day I collapsed and could not get out of bed for room service. I was sure they would fire me and once again a senior manager at the hotel visited my room and I explained that even though I swam every day to regain my strength after 30 days and a few hours of sleep every night I was exhausted. Japanese soldiers never shirk their duty, fail to take their post and in some way I explained this with tears hovering, and the manager said not to worry that he would work it out. I completed that summers work with more than sufficient money to continue my second year at New York University, School of Accounts and Finance.

My relationship with women has made a major contribution and difference in my life. The effective date of my divorce was February 05, 1979 [process began in early 1977]. My relationship with my second [and current] wife began on June 30, 1978.

In 1976, or around that time, my then current girlfriend, my son Peter, my daughter Nicole, were ascending the mountain ranges at Franconia, New Hampshire, toward Haystack and Little Haystack and beyond. We were all in excellent physical condition as we climbed easily for the two and a half to three hours required to reach the summit. We had forgotten that as we ascend the air becomes colder and thinner. At the top, we passed a hut where travelers can stay the night and eat excellent simple meals. Beyond was a trail which led from one mountain range to another. People working as part of the Franconia mountain ranges carry as much as fifty to seventy pounds in back-packs: extraordinary what a person can carry on their back and more extraordinary what mankind can carry in their mind, a universe of travails.

An attractive determined and official sounding female forest ranger approached us, came to about six to eight inches from my face and in a very commanding voice said, "I want you to take your entire family off this mountain now. We are expecting a drop in the temperature of at least twenty degrees in the next hour and the temperature will drop considerably after that. Do you understand what I am saying?" I said, "Yes" and she quickly turned around to speak with some other people who had just reached the summit. I knew that with her determination and dedication to her job, once she had told me what was important, she would not look back but would continue to inform other people of the dangerous weather conditions which were imminent.

I quickly darted forward toward a large rock to block her vision of our movement along the summit trail. In checking in with my family, everyone seemed ready to go on and to continue the brisk pace. Somehow, I missed the turn-off going down which was from my past recollection less than a quarter of a mile from where we were standing. When we finally started our descent, I could already feel the drop in temperature the forest ranger had spoken of. I realized then that everyone was dressed in shorts; we had no warm clothing or food, and then I remembered that I didn't even have a flashlight. I had endangered my entire family; they were clearly going to be in harm's way because of my obstinacy.

We were walking down a trail, but it was not one familiar to me. With the sun setting and the temperature dropping, we were literally in the dark, with only the moon glow to light our way. My child asked, "Dad, do you need a flashlight?" I was angry when they said that as I thought they were joking, but they pulled out a large black flashlight saying, "When I left the tent I thought we might need this, Dad, right?" Their foresight saved our lives. At that moment I realized I was responsible for our predicament, and I was going to be first down the trail, no matter what. When a Samurai makes a fatal error, his life is expendable and all amends and appropriate actions must be taken. There clearly, inevitably, was no issue or question about this action. When I pointed the flashlight back up the steep hill we'd just descended, I saw the markings on the uphill side of the trail and knew we were heading the right way; this definitely was the operative trail, even if it did not look familiar … but in the dark everything looks different. Somehow, as we descended, we must have moved into the downhill trail I was intending to use. We soon reached an area where some trees were partially submerged in wetland, while other trees appeared to be rotted ten to twelve feet above their bases, with no leaves or branches, as if they had died from some disease. I realized that we were in the middle of a bog and unless we got out of that area quickly we would suffer from hyperthermia or some other deadly condition. My first step after that submerged my left foot about two feet into a quickening muddy substance. Everyone rushed to pull me out. girlfriend was furious at me and rightly so; I felt guilty and ashamed at my behavior. It was clear that my life was expendable, that I needed to step forward and take full responsibility. I was both angry and ashamed. These mixed confluences of feelings were tempered in silence until I said, "We are close to the road; we will be there soon now." While I made this reassuring remark I did not believe it completely, but I knew the road was close (I could hear cars in the distance) and so was our tent.

I am not clear what occurred next, other than I was immediately aware of a full moon, my child holding my hand intermittently and knowing that the higher powers were wanted and needed. I believe that I turned my life over to God and asked for his help, fully accepting there were consequences for my foolish and impetuous behavior. If a life had to be forfeited I asked that it be mine and that my family be saved.

Cars now seemed to be rushing by as the wind swept their droning sound towards us, but we could not see any lights or road, just nothing. We knew we were close to the road, but could not find it. Once again I had attempted to prove something, but it was not a contribution, it did not farther the quality of people's lives, and it almost caused the death of the members of my family. I recognized finally that such behavior was dangerous and I vowed that from that moment on I would listen, listen, listen, as was the byword at the Center of the Light, to others and be guided by right action. Interesting how I could hear the guiding voice about other people's lives, but I refused to engage in right action in my own life, as if I turned off my common sense and reasoning. I know that out of that evening's experience I seriously damaged my relationship with my girlfriend, and no amount of apology really made a difference.

There are times in one's life when one's actions cause permanent, indelible scars of separation. One cannot go back in time and reverse one's actions; one can only accept the actions, behavior, attitude, way of being, words one used, and take heed, so that future life events will be tempered by what one has learned.

I was genuinely sad that I had damaged my relationship with my family and could only use my life from that moment on as a series of actions to farther the quality of others' lives. I also asked for God's forgiveness and forbearance. When I had a moment after my family settled down in the tent, I had a catharsis, a tear shed to let go of my transgression. "God grant me the power to accept the things I cannot change, to change the things I can and the wisdom to know the difference."

Our mutual ongoing silence about these harrowing events seemed to cauterize the wound made by this life threatening event. Silence does not close an unwelcome door of experience; however; one must complete hidden fears and concerns and to continue to take responsibility for breakdowns.

Each difficult traumatizing life event requires one to go back and examine the experience and acknowledge one's wrongdoing and ask for understanding and forgiveness. One must attempt to reconcile differences by accepting and not defending, by listening and not talking, and by engaging latent content and body language. Then, by specific action, one must demonstrate with consistency and aplomb appropriate action; otherwise, one repeats dangerous and threatening behavior as a revolving cycle further damaging the world and the people we love.

When one is uncertain about one's behavior, one must ask others – partners, family, friends, even acquaintances – "What's so in this situation?" People usually have good directional finders about life's vicissitudes, even when explaining an experience in which they took no part.

In seeking a greater understanding of dilemmas, conflicts, separation issues, or confusing experiences, it is not helpful to blame and project and assign fault elsewhere. What's important is to get feedback from others, a process which begins true introspection and changing patterns in one's life.

Until one is responsible for one's actions there is only withholding and denial, avoidance and camouflaging the facts that will set one free from compromising and dangerous behavior.

Charles: The Training of Ph.D. Hypnotherapists

———— ❧ ————

During one workshop, I had cleared an executive who invited only one person, Charles, indicating he was a friend and gave no further information about him; he would not play a part in her evening but would just be a friend and observer. I had, as was my practice, been praying for someone who was teaching hypnotherapy to accept me as a hypnotherapy intern.

At the end of the evening Charles came over to me and said, "You are extraordinary. What is your Ph.D. in?" I said I had no doctorate, just an undergraduate degree in psychology and business and was going to pursue a degree as an MSW. He then disclosed the following: "Did you know that XX was on psychotropic medications and is schizophrenic? I am her therapist." I was greatly un-nerved by what he said. He went on to say that my interventions were careful, gentle and supportive. While he broke her anonymity he assumed I was aware of her history as this was an integral part of the clearing process which customarily lasted about 3 hours.

I kept asking myself why I had no inkling of her mental status or condition, of her having been in treatment for an extended period of time. I was careful in my screening process and asked pointed questions; she had evaded the truth, since she would have had to furnish a release from her therapist to participate. Thereafter, in a very brief conversation, he said he trained Ph.D. hypnotherapists in a one day a week internship program. I asked if I might talk with him farther about my participating in that program and he said he only accepted PhD's, but that at the very least we could have lunch and I took his business card.

Some weeks later I became one of his interns, and on Thursdays, I would arrive at his office mid-day and act as a receptionist unless I was invited into sessions with the permission of his patient. My day ended about 8:00 or 9:00 pm.

There came a time when I sensed he was going to die and I asked him at the end of one evening about his health; he was rather abrupt and gave a quick abbreviated answer which was uncommon for him. Several months later he passed away very unexpectedly.

When another intern and I were helping his wife do some supportive activities at his private home after her husband had passed away, we were sitting in their back yard eating lunch, and she said to me, "You know, I knew he was going to die." I was shocked that she said this, but spoke of my having had the same sense although there were no tell-tale signs or indications of any health issue. We both attempted to trace how it was that we had similar impressions and could identify no signs or symptoms that we could attribute to this strange phenomena of our natural knowing. She said that she was not aware of any other such impression in her life-time, nor was I: this was a first for both of us. I had heard of such experiences from my mother, who said that when her mother died, she saw her in a mirror when she passed a dresser. Her mother was a great distance from where my mother was located. My mother also predicted the deaths of several people in my father's life; this kind of reporting, according to my mother, was always a source of conflict and consternation for my father; however, I was never privileged to those experiences personally that occurred between them.

The Fire Island Sea Prayer

As I sat on the deck of my ocean-front leased home in Fire Island, New York, typing chapters for the Samurai Gypsy or the Gypsy Samurai, I recalled the miracle of channeling energy to a higher power of clairvoyance. In the middle of the summer of 1978 I met my future, second wife. It was what many people on Fire Island called a summer island romance, and they usually last for only one or part of one season. From the time I first danced with her on that fateful night in June, we have been together both in the city and our summer home.

The summer we met I was single sharing a singles house with brothers; a seven bedroom two story stick-built summer home. The inside walls were cypress that had been brought from the owner's North Carolina property many years earlier. The house was built by a regional figure-head, a spiritual curmudgeon, a self-made man. He could be brilliant, charming, worldly, inspired and at the drop of a hat he could transform to a 'landlord,' directing, disciplining and making strong concerted demands. On Fire Island he was a hero and maverick; he set the mold for being 'his own man.'

When I danced with my future second wife that magical night I left my share house and moved in with her at her house in Long Island. I'll never forget my first morning as I entered the kitchen area. Long standing friends had more or less purchased full shares for this five bedroom house and those in the kitchen had no idea who I was or that I was there. One of the house organizers asked if I wanted coffee or a roll or both. I searched for a single roll amongst fifty in a garbage bag that occupied the entire top surface of the refrigerator. This prosperous New York singles group, was a drop-in Island spot for anyone who was someone. The sequel to this incident was being invited to have a drink. "What do you have?" I asked. Their response was, "Whatever you like. Check out the linen closet over there." What I didn't know was that their liquor shipment had arrived just the day before and every shelf was stacked five or six deep. There were eight or so shelves and the floor held larger bottles. It was like a liquor store, not a liquor closet. That's when I knew I was out of my league: the liquor bill alone was probably more than I would spend for a share for the entire season. My future wife always commented that when she entered the house she had her checkbook open. This experience was extravagance beyond my wildest imagination: I loved this new reality of abundance and sharing.

The following summer we decided to go to a smaller community. We found a little 'tiffany' house; everything sparkled. The community was very quiet with no movie theater, only one prominent restaurant and several basic stores, i.e., general store, liquor store, market. We knew very early in the season that this would be a one-season experience and that we both missed the house nearer the beach with closer proximity to a major town with restaurants, a movie theater and discos.

In late July to early August I began calling places, still hoping for a suitable house to rent for next year. Every time I called a realty agent they had either just left with a potential renter, were on the way back to the office, or a machine took my message and promised a call back. During the next several weeks (almost Labor Day - the end of the season) I made at least five to six calls.

No one seemed to respond and that was an indicator to me of some form of resistance, either mine or outside forces. I then began to pray more intensely each weekend until a message came through which was a customary way for me to channel incoming near future experiences.

While I was growing up, life events always seemed to have a 'déjà vu' quality, but seldom in the here and now, always in the there and then, and I wondered if I was imagining or making up these recalled experiences at future dates, as if I had been there and done that. The voice 'told' me to wait until 4:00 P.M on a specified Saturday and call the landlord of the house for an opening. At precisely 4:00 P.M. I called and the landlord's son (also a real estate agent) and he answered the phone, sounding as if he had just run to the phone. I expressed an interest in a house on the beach and would consider the bay. I expressed reservations knowing there were few houses available in on the beach since renters returned year after year as it was one of the most preferred sections of the island because of its seclusion, trees and owner's thoroughbred horses (brought up from his North Carolina estate). My future wife was standing close by to listen in case there were any interesting opportunities. At that moment the landlord said it was interesting. He had just come back from his father's and a house had opened up. He described the house that I had been in and had been leased for at least ten years by the same people. I said the house he was describing belonged to these people and it didn't seem possible that they would not take it for another season. He indicated that they were not going to rent and both the top and the bottom of the house were open for rental and asked if I were interested. I said I would take it on the spot and asked if he needed a contract or a binder. He said he needed neither, just my commitment and an arranged time for us to see the house together the following weekend.

The following weekend we trekked 1 ½ miles to see the house. When we arrived the house looked like a pit. The landlord said he had just taken 17 bags of garbage out of the house which seemed unbelievable. There were cracked dried eggs in the refrigerator and directly beneath its door, single sneakers were also in the fridge and clothes were strewn about in almost every room as if the occupants needed to make a quick get-away. My wife was adamant that she would not live in such a place, no matter how many seasons I had spent in this house, regardless of the ocean being directly in front of the house or the fact that there were no houses bordering three sides (which is quite unusual for Fire Island living). Somehow I convinced my future wife that after the place was cleaned up it would look fantastic and she supported my foretelling of the future. I started out in this house as a half-share with my two children from a previous marriage, sharing four of the nine weekends, an unheard of contract in a totally singles house - yet another miracle.

Knowing when to tune into the universe and listen, listen, listen is a magic that has ebbed and flowed in my life, a life force providing countless blessings for me, my family, and others: I thank God for these many blessings. The answers are always present in the universe and our lives and just need to be called forth. Like the penguins who have not learned of our predatory nature, they walk side by side with man. It is important that we listen to the inner workings of aligning our needs with some higher power that reaches out when we tune in. The nature of this force, the constancy, the permanence is elusive and never ever constant. One's practice is to gather such forces within one's true self and merge with the truths that are ever present in the life force. To believe in the inherent voice of revelation causes it to come into existence.

God grant me the power to listen and to pay attention to the thoughts and sensations, the feelings that are always there to be heard; at times to listen to silence and find an answer that is precisely waiting to respond to our needs is entangled in a secret web of confusions. It would appear to be only our belief that our interests are contributory and in alignment with some greater power other than going to the wishing well and half heartedly, so to speak, getting our wish of wishes.

When I prayed, I prayed to the sun forces and formed a triangle with both hands tightly clasped together extended to the sun. This was a channeling rod, maybe a divining rod to cradle and direct the energy and forces of being into having and knowing: Fire Island Sea Prayer.

The Exorcism

Pete Faust, a distinguished New York City attorney and entrepreneur who had graduated first in his class at Harvard, participated in the Money Workshop produced by a communication corporation. I was the last to apply, had clearly the least amount of financial resources, and generally was outclassed by assets, capital and knowledge base although I had graduated in the top 25% of my class at St. John's University Graduate School, in both Finance and Operations Research.

They coined our group the 'Million Dollar Club'. Fortunately, a number of the participants knew me as a workshop leader and someone committed to transformation, miracles and supporting positive changes in people's lives, those were my winning calling cards. Pete and Glen were fortuitously my inside lobby. The workshop participants had to vote on adding one more member because, as I recall it, the group had already met one time. There was one dissenter, and since it was a group in many ways reserved for millionaires, my chances of being accepted seemed slim, to say the very least. It seemed that the huddle was taking place and I was jumping up at their perimeter screaming, "Pick-me - pick-me," and whatever the quarterback called was the next play - like you're in or you're out. I was voted in.

We met once a week for approximately six months. As part of this workshop each person had an evening and soon it was my turn. This was the night to make declarations, ask for support, and utilize the collective financial strength and insight of this millionaire group to determine what impediments might be in my way to being more successful in my pursuits of wealth, abundance and prosperity in life (not necessarily restricted to dollars and cents intentions or interests).

There was a pre-screening meeting or two with the workshop leader to prepare and review my agenda, define my needs and assessments, and in general work toward an efficient utilization of time and interests with the group. Since I had been a particularly contributory player adding intuitive and psychological insight and interventions that at times were breakthrough in nature, I knew I would be powerfully contributed too. As I recall, there were some seventeen members in this Money Workshop. My wife, children and friends were invited, as was the practice for our evening. It was to be a soul-searching evening that moved one's judgment and insight toward achieving prosperity and abundance and as well discovering and strategizing action plans to remedy patterns of blocked energy. I had played hard-ball with the group, as we all did, and no one was willing to let me skirt an issue or evade looking at a truth which kept me stuck in dependent behavior with the incumbent financial restraints.

Just prior to my evening, which was mid-point in the workshop calendar, I had offered my Breakthrough Experience (a one-day, one-on-one healing intensive) to Pete. I indicated that he could pay me whatever he felt the experience was worth and that he would be the judge of the value he derived. Being a man of integrity, Pete said he was uncomfortable with this agreement since he felt that the process could be invaluable and the fee he would assign could be all of his financial holdings or maybe even more. The tightness of the group and the collective integrity of the group deepened each member's experience wanting success for each other: there was an all-for-one and one-for-all camaraderie. So I determined $250 as the fee for the session and we agreed.

As we began working together, my Breakthrough Experience did not seem to work. I needed to reach deeper inside my psychic and psychological knowledge to extricate truths that would be both contributory and contributory to Pete's shift in his highly intended life goals.

My Money Workshop session began precisely on time and my experience was that there seemed to be many more people attending. As I began my agenda by reading my goals for the three hour session, Pete stepped forward and made the following announcement.

"Before George starts his evening, I want to make an offer that will make a contribution to your lives. The night before last George did his Breakthrough Experience process with me. I was offered the process on the basis that whatever I felt the process was worth was what I should pay. Fortunately, I decided to pay his stipulated fee rather than agree to his proposal. Were I to have agreed to his proposal, I would have to pay him no less than one million dollars, and that would not have been enough. Let me say that where he goes to get what he knows is a place few people have uncovered. This was and is the greatest one-to-one experience of my entire life. Clearly it has changed my life and how I perceive and understand myself. This is my offer to everyone in this room: I want everyone to participate in this Breakthrough Experience and anyone who is not 100% satisfied will be 100% refunded. I personally guarantee this experience. Just send your secretary to my office and my secretary will cut you a check or call me."

He proceeded, in his special way, to enroll every member of the money workshop and every other person present. I had twenty six enrollees entered into my calendar. For me his testimonial and sanction with a personal guarantee was difficult to accept. From these beginnings I performed some 189 individual processes with key principals and vice presidents representing major corporations.

Pete had his fiancée Dolly do the BE process. I invited Denise Ciento to my slightly off Park Avenue apartment and so began the story of the exorcism. I knew Deniese was a novitiate in a convent, the most austere and difficult Catholic order for nuns as she describe it, and had not been ordained; and I vaguely recall that only two novitiates were eligible, she and another of long standing. This order had very stringent requirements, no heat, no hot water, all habits had to be hand washed and ironed personally. There were long arduous chores and the duty in service to Jesus was asceticism. Denise did not complain. She revealed her experiences simply that this was the way it was and this order required such behavior and responsible commitment to a challenging service. Nevertheless, Denise left the order because, from her point of view, it seemed she would not be ordained under any circumstances, regardless of her painstaking efforts to devote herself relentlessly to her tasks and God.

As we began the session, there seemed to me to be a very heavy aura in the room. I sensed that there was 'gloom and doom' in our presence that emanated from a source other than our combined essences. I started several times, and then for the first and only time I have ever made such a made such a request, I said we need to leave this house immediately and find a sanctuary, some religious site in the immediate area. To my mind's way of visualizing reality, it was late in the day, it was dark, and I was clearly unfamiliar with any churches, rectories or even synagogues that might consider such a request. Why would they?

I went to two religious sites on Lexington Avenue. The first was a building that lodged nuns for the Archdiocese and the second church was Old Souls, neither of which wanted to consider my request. What I recall saying next was that I needed to do some work with my client and I needed a religious sanctuary. I said nothing about Denise's background or the intentions of the process. We made almost a 360-degree circle until we were at the corner of 80th and Park Avenue. That's when I said to Denise, you must know a place that we might go to. At that moment she became somewhat concerned and mildly aggravated. She said, "First, I come to your home, and then we go from one church setting to another and now you tell me I should know of a place. This is all becoming pretty far-fetched."

I must admit that even I was beginning to doubt the reality of my actions and request. This experience was becoming strange.

Had I lost touch with reality? Was I completely deranged? It was the darkest of nights and it was cold and biting, stinging my ears and hands. Neither of us was properly dressed this weather.

I reiterated, "Remember way back-there is some place that you are familiar with in this very neighborhood where we can go and do our process." At that very moment I could see from her facial expression that she completely doubted my abilities and wanted to leave. She was about to hail a cab, she headed toward incoming south bound traffic. Even I couldn't say she was not absolutely right in her actions. But then after a silent moment when critical decisions are kindling, in the last stages of formulation, she said, "My God I went to a Catholic school near here, only a few blocks away, Loyola, Loyola that's it."

I breathed a sigh of relief. Again, I broached my skepticism: a Catholic church-would they entertain such a request or ask us to leave post haste?

We entered a very large complex and I noticed a silver bowl inset into the stone wall, filled with holy water. We blessed ourselves, as we were both Catholic. I approached the desk and asked the woman behind a glass partition if I could use on their rooms to do a process. She briefly asked me about the process and I stated that the Breakthrough Experience was a transformational New Age experience lasting about three hours and that for some reason I needed a sanctuary and that it had to be a church [though personally I did not have any understanding why it needed to be a church]. She said that I would need to secure permission from a priest who was having a private session with a member of their church. Were I willing to wait, I could speak to Father

X personally. She indicated for both of us to go upstairs and be seated outside his office until his session was over. We waited about twenty minutes and after a woman left the room, we reverently entered.

I explained our needs carefully and confirmed we were both of the Catholic faith. The priest asked many questions to determine if our work was in keeping with his church doctrine. I asked for sanctuary, a strange word as I recall back to that time. The details of that meeting are unclear, other than the priest allows us to use one of several rooms downstairs.

Praise be to God. God had intervened and blessed my work, our work, the work that would begin shortly. My fears were great and my own disbelief in this journey strong, but then somehow my-our-guidance system was working with God's guidance. The priest walked us to the corridor and blessed our work together.

The room we entered with the help of the woman that had initially referred us to the priest was entirely paneled in a dark paneled wood, light was dim, and adjoined Park Avenue on the first floor. There was a six-foot oak table, a wooden Christ figure was on the wall, and there was an ambiance of serenity and tranquility. It was a comforting feeling to be in this room. I felt safe, secure and protected. Curious, I asked my self, "Why 'protected'?" At that moment, from some inward instinctively directed reason, I said I needed holy water, a wooden cross of Christ and rosary beads. I excused myself and went to the front desk and asked the same lady who had directed us initially. She gave me a set of her own rosary beads and said they were especially blessed and were sanctified. Somehow, she seemed to know much more than she was saying, yet all she did say was very accommodating and supportive and requested that I not question her any farther. She said that the rosary was extremely valuable to her as they had been in her family a long time and she was particularly insistent that I return them before she left and I agreed.

The hour was now late. As I could clearly see on her face, Denise was apprehensive. I asked her if she had any idea or knowledge why these circumstances evidenced themselves in her case and she said no, she had no idea. This was definitely different from any other Breakthrough Experience.

I began to ask her certain questions. Quite early in the session she said, "You know my mother superior indicated sometime before I left that she felt that I was possessed by Satan, but then I suppose you already know this."

"Why would you suppose I would know this?"

"Since you're a psychic I just assumed you knew and that was why we were taking all these precautions - a sanctified place, holy water, a priest's sanction to use the church, being within the confines of a church, like that, it just seemed you knew."

"When would you have told me that you were thought to be possessed by the forces of Satan?"

"Well, I didn't say I was, but that's what she said."

"Have you had any callings from Satan or omens of evil?" I truly don't recall what she said thereafter. Our Breakthrough Experience process began. I remembered an incantation which was been given to me by a Reverend which was, "I cover thee in the blood of Jesus and Satan be gone." I said this several times and the statement felt somewhat out of sorts to me, strange to my tongue and understanding in this world. I believe I said this phrase three times and shortly after, Denise claimed that there had been a lifting of a weight or pressure or influence that had weighed heavily upon her while in the convent and at other times in her service to Christ.

I was somewhat pressured, challenged and thwarted by this experience and felt that the process was almost over. She said "Did you see that? Did you see that? A presence, a powerful presence went out of that window just now. Did you see it?" Just before she said that, the hair on my arms were standing straight up, and while there seemed to be an energy force moving, it was not as clear to me as it was to Denise.

I proceeded to return the objects to the lady at the reception desk, but was advised she had left for the night. It was suggested I call the following day and arrange a mutually convenient time to return her personal effects. The next day I called only to have forgotten her name. She said to drop by around five and she would be there. As I entered the rectory, she quickly greeted me.

Her first words were, "How did the exorcism go?"

I still remember the chill that ran throughout my body. I responded, "What exorcism?" "The one you performed last night. You asked for all the accoutrements for an exorcism. You know it is really strange because I seldom work that late and never on Friday nights. That is not a night I volunteer. I was asked to help out in a personal circumstance and made an exception. As I recall it is the only Friday I ever assisted. I gave you those holy beads because you needed a strong healing channel. Those rosary beads have never been used in the past," implying for other exorcisms I guess, though I did not question her statement.

She realized that I had no knowledge and warned me, cautioned me to never again do such work without consulting those who were knowledgeable about such work. She gave me the address of a priest to write and I did. His letter was shocking for it not only cautioned me to stop such work, which I again had no idea I was engaged in, but that the dangers to me were very real and could penetrate the core of my life and my health and that I could become possessed. The substance of that letter, which I search for today, scorched my mind with fear and dilemma.

How could I have engaged in such work without proper prior knowledge and training and why didn't Joshua warn me accordingly [Joshua is the voice that speaks through me]? While there were two other incidents, one with a minister in upstate New York, and another with a friend's husband Conn., I have intentionally avoided the perils of such work which I completely acknowledge should be left to appropriate clergy, proper sites and locations where exorcisms are sanctioned by the church.

Curiously, Denise had been directly responsible for bringing me to the Center of the Light where I studied and graduated from their two-year holistic training program, including herbs-nutrition – massage – foot reflexology – and spiritual development.

Praise the Lord for watching and protecting me and for bringing such powerful people into my life experience.

Every word and experience as related here happened exactly as I reported them and I thank God for protecting me and releasing Denise from whatever restraints to her living a free life were present.

The Space of Miracles: Wainwright House

In 1982, during my final months at the Center of the Light, I had a strong and compelling desire to do a one-day seminar on the Space of Miracles. This burning desire became more and more intense as the Center of the Light June graduation date drew closer in August, 1983. I knew very little about the nature of miracles, yet the desire was pulsating, constant, saying create the Space of Miracles Workshop.

I went to the bookstore in the Village and gathered up as many books as I could find and sought other references they might recommend.

For the next several months I read and abstracted and formulated a body of knowledge that seemed to represent some semblance of knowledge about the nature, history and occurrences of miracles. Being on the Board of directors of Wainwright House facilitated my acceptance as a credible presenter.

There were about thirty-three people, mostly women, attending, as well as a small logistics team, including my wife (who was always an incredible support liaison, perhaps generating the space of Miracles as a context for me to deliver the experience. There is this 'win-win' power surge between us). Although the workshop was held in the spring, the day was cold and windy and leaves entered the outer doorway and scampered about, rustling on the stone floor every time the front door to the building opened.

The seminar was principally didactic. The attendees shared their experiences openly and clearly, and there was a cohesiveness and magnetic spontaneity to this group. The participants seemed to be one floating floral arrangement with many interconnected petals, each petal representing another member of this group's essence.

Perhaps some ten minutes from the end of the workshop, well after our lunch and approaching three or four in the afternoon, Frank burst into the room. The wind gusting as the front door opened made it look as if a tail wind had pushed him into the room with tremendous velocity. He used both hands to close the door. He was wearing a green shiny hooded winter coat, with bone tie clasps and threaded loops. His interruption was unexpected and the group was taken aback. As he approached me, with the participants listening classroom style, he asked, "Am I too late to get my healing? You remember. I have cancer and you promised me a healing." I was dumbfounded. I knew Frank from groups we attended at a seminar training, but I honestly did not recall ever offering to do a healing and absolutely not for cancer, not me. I asked Frank to be seated, to take off his jacket and remain quiet until I completed the workshop. The workshop participants were adaptive but confused. When I finished the content of the workshop, I asked the group if they would be willing to collectively do a healing. My guidelines were that at no time did anyone have to touch Frank and that if one member in the workshop felt it was not appropriate to do such a group healing, we would end the workshop.

Everyone chose to be at cause for a miracle - a healing - to take place. I believe I admitted to the group that I honestly did not recall offering Frank the healing, but then the universe provides extraordinary opportunities. I was mildly upset that I'd made such an offer and could not recall doing so. My memory was intact and I would not have been casual about offering a healing since I had never healed cancer, and had no inkling what it would involve. Also, this was a "first" workshop and such a happening would be beyond my notions of the Space of Miracles at that time. Nevertheless, I did take time to engage my natural knowing center and to ask the question, "Is such a healing appropriate or not?" The answer was that it was. In a short prayer I asked for God's intervention to heal Frank.

I asked the group to make one large circle around Frank. I recalled that I had Tibetan bells in my carry-all bag. I directed one member of the group to make eye contact with Frank, and for the entire group to maintain silence at all times. When they heard the chime of the Tibetan bells, the group was to move counter-clockwise, one position to the right, so that another person was in eye contact with Frank. I asked Frank if there was anything he needed to say to the group. "Yes, I am trying to recall how you invited me here, and it is not clear to me, since I intended to be part of the workshop and got a very late start. My doctor reports that I have terminal cancer and only six months to live. I believe in you, George, and in the Space of Miracles. I believe something will happen here that will change my relationship to my cancer."

I began the process with a short prayer and, while I can't recall the exact words, the context of the prayer follows closely: "God, guide each and every one of us gathered here today, for when two or more are gathered in your name, we may beseech thee to call upon your love and healing powers to alter our pain, suffering and diseases. We ask that there be a healing today for Frank and that your blessings and bountiful gifts be made available to each and every person here today and in the world we live in."

The thirty or so members of the Space of Miracles workshop moved like a large, well regulated clock, with dedicated precision time and time and time again. The external sounds of the world became absolutely silent. As each person in turn faced Frank in the silent room, their eyes filled with compassion and sometimes tears, and the process went on and on and on until they had completed one full circle, one time only for every member of the group.

About a week later, Frank, called me at work. He said, "Hi, this is Frank, have you ever heard of spontaneous remission, George?" I said "Yes." "Well I went to my doctor and they say they can't explain what happened, but that I no longer have cancer and the only way they can explain it is to say I have experienced spontaneous remission. So, George, your Space of Miracles does produce Miracles." It was difficult to remain engaged in the conversation. I never saw or heard from Frank again; he lived about five blocks from my old residence in New York City.

I had been driven to Wainwright House by one of the members of the first graduating class from the Center of the Light while my wife held my hand in the back seat. On the way up, I kept saying, "I know nothing about Miracles. This workshop is a mistake. I'm going to make a fool of myself." I prayed that God would forgive my arrogance, for I meant no disrespect; why I am called at times to take certain actions truly confuses me. I am compelled, challenged, transported to be and to know things. My wife was reassuring, as is her way, as I continued to cry in the back seat. I began weeping uncontrollably, and declaring that my workshop was going to be a failure and how could I ever believe a mortal could in any way describe the 'space of miracles.'

Perhaps, only perhaps, sometimes in life one is challenged to be outrageous, to engage a subject, an action, a belief that begins a life-time journey. We must acknowledge our fears and issues of conflict as this creates the opening to create out of nothing, for nothing is just another position that describes everything. Hopefully, those journeys are filled with integrity, honesty, and a desire to make a difference in the lives of other people. As a social worker I believe I am an advocate for positive change in the lives of others. From my perspective, life is to be lived as a brilliant star ascending into the universe, always reaching for distant galaxies of attainment and always moving to a new orbit of realizations and enlightenment. If I serve you I serve myself. If I only serve myself, I remove the presence of the other and abandon my relationship to love and forgiveness which is the foundation of being aligned to the world I live in.

Seeing is Believing

—◦◦◦—

While I was on the Board of Directors at Wainwright House, in the mid 1980's, I attended a major Saturday event. I was seated among a group of three or four women and the woman on my right was transmitting information.

I asked, "May I have your permission to share some intuitive information with you?"

She said, "It depends a lot on what you want to say." The presentation had ended and people were beginning to disperse in small clusters moving to the main house as the presentation had been made on the lawn.

"What I want to share is about your glasses."

"My glasses, what about my glasses?" she responded, somewhat annoyed.

"I apologize, please forgive me."

"Well, now that you have begun, why don't you complete what you want to say? Who are you?"

After a brief introduction, she was less upset about my intrusion and asked me to share whatever impressions I might have. "I believe that the glasses you are wearing are not correctly prescribed. They are new glasses, aren't they?"

"Yes", pausing, "yes, they are, but there is nothing wrong with my glasses. I have been wearing them since Thursday."

The event we were attending was held on Saturday of the same week. "I believe your right lens needs to be reevaluated."

She said, "How do you know that, are you a doctor or optometrist?"

I explained that Wainwright House was erected on a special site and information was more readily accessible to sensitives there than in other areas. The woman was in her fifties, attired in a one piece fashionable dress, and definitely a woman of means. "Remember when you first started to wear your glasses you were complaining they were too strong and your eyes started to tear. And now, from time to time, especially when you begin to wear your glasses at the start of your day, your eyes feel strained and your focus is not that clear in your right eye."

She paused for a very long time, looking across the water and the other women were silent and attentive. "My God, you are right. Since I have been wearing these glasses, I have been having trouble with my vision. I simply thought that what was required was time for me to get adjusted to my new prescription. Thank you for helping me, thank you; I might have done irreparable damage had you not sat next to me at my table. God bless you, George."

There was very little said after that and I moved away, wondering if I had really made a contribution or that I had convinced someone of my belief. She said there was still time that afternoon to have another eye examination to determine if the lenses were correctly prescribed or not. Once the woman felt that my contribution was sincere, that my apology was from the heart about intruding into her life and that Wainwright House was indeed a center for healing and transformation, she was willing to receive. I also realized I needed to address my body readings in such a way as to cause less resistance.

For an individual to accept a healing, they need to be accepting of new information and willing to trust and empower another's transfer of healing energy.

Designation as A Messenger of God

While serving as a contributory member of Wainwright House, I observed that they needed a variety of services. At that time my association with many professionals that owned companies in the building trades, electrical and heating made it possible for me to ask for some time with the Board, to offer them the pro-bono services of a group of professionals willing to contribute to a worthy organization. The principal areas of contribution would not be in spirituality or seminars or in the refinement of their select, long-standing programs, but in enhancements to their physical facility. During the meeting that Saturday morning our anticipated contributions were short lived, once we realized that the specializations we had to offer did not match their then current needs. I was never quite sure if their concerns involved the battery of professionals who in the main owned their own The name is derived from Latin roots companies and served other major corporations in New York City or if they felt I was an outsider looking in and not really grasping what was needed and wanted; perhaps they thought I was ineffective in leading the focus group. I felt a great loss in this experience, first because I had inconvenienced the support group that gave up a good part of their Saturday, and secondly because the meeting seemed to go flat when the group began to extol my need to make a contribution.

At a prior meeting I had engaged in a conversation as to what I might be able to contribute to Wainwright; I believe this ultimately led to the meeting with the select board. Someone said at some point, "You know there is a name for people like you. I have never met one before, but they refer to you as a messenger of God." He proceeded to explain briefly what such a person represented and it was not possible for me to engage in the conversation or to understand what I had done to warrant his statement. I did feel acknowledged and felt that since he was an ordained minister from a prominent Ivy League school some important distinction was being made.

For years thereafter, messages would come to me and I would need to deliver them. The first few messages I delivered were very threatening to me as I feared that the person who I asked permission to share the message with would be so infuriated or threatened that they would perhaps challenge me openly or even attack me.

One experience in particular was most provoking and fear-ridden. I was attending the New School of Social Research at the graduate level preparing for their Ph.D. program, taking a symposium course in which four professors were seated on a dais in the auditorium where the student audience numbered well over 200 students discussing central themes in psychology. One student usually came in late, would be boisterously argumentative, then leave in a huff. I seldom understood what he said, since his references and apparent sophistication was well beyond my academic comprehension, but the professors seemed to engage his questions, even though at times it seemed to me that he was acting in an unstable manner. Quite often I wondered why they did not either expel him or at least give him some form of warning as his interruptions were confusing and he didn't seem to contribute to the lecture, but perhaps it was just my inability to understand his intended contribution.

The voice gave me a message to deliver to him. Did the voice come from nowhere and say do this or do that? The answer is, not exactly. Was there some ritual, occurrence, or structure during these incoming messages? The answer again is, not exactly. When information came through, the message would periodically repeat itself until I delivered the information. It was not an identifiable voice and it came at random in no specific and prescribed way. It was like telling oneself "Don't forget to get sugar and milk tonight." I never knew the individual I was instructed to deliver the information to. I never felt there would be some punitive outcome if I did not deliver the information or that there would be some consequences or issues if I did not deliver the message. The messages were not necessarily complex or multi-faceted: they were usually straightforward regarding some specific issue in a person's life; perhaps I could say some information that would alter some important aspect of their life.

If I did not want to deliver the message, it was given to me three or four times; this was the case with the graduate student whom I passed on the street at different locations throughout the city. I felt it was not possible to avoid telling him, because he would appear again and again. I was walking around 81st Street and sure enough there he was, walking straight toward me. I gathered my courage because I thought for sure he would attack me physically if I delivered the message. I stopped him, introduced myself as a fellow student in the doctors program at the New School and he was welcoming. (I was actually not in the program at that time, but was attempting to acquire sufficient graduate credits to apply for the doctorate program, and was literally years away from being eligible for consideration.) I then asked for permission to report information as a "messenger of God." Calling myself a Messenger of God seemed frightening, inaccurate, and untrue: "Who sir me sir? No sir not I sir. Then sir who sir?" as the rhyme goes. I felt I was a lie, an imposter, that such messages from God are not possible in this world. Never ever had anyone I met revealed they were delivering messages from God. However, the graduate student appeared stable, not compromised or facially offended by my offering, open and engaging, and asked me, "Please tell me what I need to know." I went into some altered state and gave him the information. I was unsure how he would react and actually stood back, anticipating the worst. I was more than a little frightened of what his reaction would be. I wanted to run away but was frozen, not knowing what reaction awaited me. Later I said to myself, "If I can deliver this message to this man, I can deliver God's message to any one." When he heard his message, he said, "I have been waiting for this information all of my life and I shall be indebted to you for my entire life." He went into his wallet and pulled out a card and said, "If at any time I can do anything for you, just call on me and it shall be done." I learned later that he was an important figure in the world of psychology, but I have long since misplaced his card. Such messages are delivered without any expectation of a reward, acknowledgment or recompense. It is not appropriate to ask for any gift or payment; the messenger just delivers the information and moves on. Where this belief came from I have no idea; it simply seems as if the "job" was in the telling, without expecting anything or gaining something as a reward. The sincerity of his words, his kind and empathic affect, touched my heart.

I knew at that moment that God loved me, that even delivering messages to a person I perceived to be dangerous and disturbed was God's deliverance, that I was only a messenger, simply wind or air, or sky or sea, or land or movement, and one does not argue with or fight against nature and its incalculable contribution. The messages, none of which I can recall afterwards, have nothing to do with dying, death, dismemberment, tragedy or some frightening near-term event; they are about living, life, the pursuit of happiness and providing information about restructuring and altering....I think.

A Prayer to Mercedes

I had run barefoot for years on the shores of Fire Island from Ocean Beach and Corneille Estates to Fair Harbor (at the Southern tip of Fire Island) and back. Over those years of not wearing running shoes, apparently I had damaged my instep on both feet. The podiatrist said that I would need foot surgery on both feet to correct the problem and remove the pain I experienced when I walked from the subway station to Jacobi Hospital where I was interning as a social worker at the Psych In-Patient Ward. By the time I reached Jacobi it was necessary to stop several times, to diminish the pain; there were tears in my eyes on many days as each step pounded bone against pavement. Once at Jacobi, the pain subsided. Returning home, I took the bus back to a different subway line avoiding the painful half-mile walk.

Each day I would, as was my custom, pray to the Holy Mother Mary to diminish the pain and to help me with my affliction. At that time I was 46 years old and in 1984 had made a career change from working in Fortune 50 Corporations with an MBA degree in Finance from St. John's University to attending New

York University's Graduate School of Social Work. As days turned into months, my prayers evolved into a picture of a four-door chocolate-brown Mercedes in excellent running condition. Needless to say neither my wife nor I could afford such a car; nevertheless, my prayers were vigilant. At some later date I did reflect on my audacity in making such a perennial prayer to the Holy Mother. Clearly, a bicycle would have sufficed nicely as I now think about this experience.

One morning as I was leaving my apartment, I heard the voice say, "This morning you will hear the sound of aerated tires on pebbles from behind you and this will be your car. Remember; be careful to listen to the aerated pebbles against the tires." I heard the message and as quickly as it was absorbed it disappeared. In the Bronx, I exited the subway to the street level and began my walk along the wide corridor four lane highway and access lanes adjacent to homes on Pelham Parkway South. The neighborhood adjoining Albert Einstein College of Medicine, Jacobi Medical Center, and The Kennedy Center was inhabited by wealthy home-owners. The homes were large and sprawling; mostly brick, and at times it almost appeared that no one lived there as the people traffic flow was almost imperceptible.

From behind me I heard the sound of a car approaching and what made it distinctive just before 8:00 A.M. in the morning was "the sound of aerated tires on pebbles coming from behind me." As I turned I saw a woman pulling into a spot in front of her home. She was driving a chocolate-brown, four-door vintage Mercedes in what would appear to be good condition. I hesitated to draw closer, for in that neighborhood approaching a woman early in the morning was not advisable. I waited till she exited her car and yelled out, "I'm an intern at Jacobi Hospital. Do you have any interest in selling your car?" At this point she had closed the door to her car and said she was giving her Mercedes to her nephew and did not want to sell it, but she took my telephone number anyway.

Some weeks later, she called me at my office at Jacobi Hospital and asked if I still had an interest in buying her car, to which I said, "YES!" It dawned on me only then that I had no idea where I would get the money. I felt very foolish.

Be careful what you ask for; you just may get it. She then said something very strange, "I will accept anything that you offer me for my car." I thought that was a very clever way to sell her car. She asked me how much I thought I could come up with. I said I would call her back shortly and that it was hard to determine the amount right there and then. I called my wife and her initial response was, "A Mercedes, we have no money for a Mercedes." The ensuing conversation with My wife proved most eventful. She called her father's good friend Roberta and we were given a loan of $5,000 for the car which was worth at least three times that amount. I called the women back and said I could pay $5,000 for the Mercedes and she said, "Is that the best you can do?" I said, "I know your car is worth much more, but that's all the money I can borrow and I can understand you probably don't want to sell it for so little money." She said, "Yes, I do. When you have the money call me, but I will need a few days before I can turn the car over to you." I was ecstatic; the Holy Mother had intervened. I gave thankful prayer.

The owner picked me up in her Mercedes after I disembarked from my usual subway stop somewhat earlier that morning. She told me she had gone to her local mechanic and asked him to tune up her car and make whatever repairs were necessary to have it in tip-top running condition. The mechanic said he thought she was selling the car and she responded she had actually found a buyer. The mechanic said, "No, no, no! This is not what you should do. You sell your car and let him take care of whatever needs to be fixed. If I put this car in good running condition, it will cost you a lot of money you don't have to pay." A short argument ensued with her mechanic, but in the end she pulled out of her glove compartment a bill from the garage for several hundred dollars' worth of recent repairs. She said, "I wanted you to have this car in top running condition, and it is."

She had asked for some of the money in cash and I was a bit anxious about that request since fifteen hundred in cash was a large sum of money for me and my wife. She drove me to her home and we sat in the vestibule, obliquely facing the door. Her home was spacious, immaculate and expensive-looking. I was very anxious about the cash which I needed to turn over and about being alone in her house. I felt a foreboding: something will happen to me here; no one knows I'm here. My internal dialogue was that I knew something strange was about to happen: I knew it.

She said, "I need to tell you something which I know you will find hard to believe." At that moment I wanted to bolt out of the door. "Here it comes," I said to myself, "What's her trick? What's her angle? God, what did I get myself into?" She said, "A week or so after you asked me whether I wanted to sell my car, I was reading in my bedroom upstairs and the Virgin Mother came to me and said, 'You must sell your car to this young man and accept whatever he can afford to pay you; you must not keep this car any longer.' She went on to say that she rushed to her mother who was downstairs watching television. She had taken a year off on personal leave as her mother was terminally till. She assured me that she was of sound mind, had a Ph.D. in English, came from a very religious Greek Orthodox family and that what she was telling me about had really happened and was not a fabrication. Her mother told her to bring the car to me that night, immediately, and to get rid of it quickly. She said that it was too late to call me that night and she would call me first thing the next morning. I said that I had been praying to the Holy Mother for a Mercedes, and I was awe struck when she related this story to me. I never saw her mother who apparently was in the house at the time.

We spent some time in silent prayer and acknowledged the power of prayer and our mutual love for the Holy Mother.

Do You know whose Voice that is?

I worked at PROMESA [Puerto Rican Organization to Motivate, Enlighten Substance Abusers] from 1989 through May 1993 as the Social Services Director for a multi-faceted community development corporation. I had survived two reorganizations. I was privileged to remain under the tutelage of the Executive Director. He included me in his personal life, some parts of his social life and most importantly included me in the Friday Morning Directors Meeting. He encouraged my contributions, placed me on committees and research groups in developing programs that had applications in a broad array of outreach programs.

There came a time in which I was extremely threatened in the third reorganization at PROMESA and felt my time had come to be fired, most of the Directors were replaced. I went for coaching with an Associate Professor at NYU while pursuing my Advanced Certificate in Social Work, the first stage toward their Ph.D. program. He considered our work together to be therapy and not coaching. In that divine intervention, not to minimize our work together, he said, "perhaps you will need to accept that you will always be impacted by your past life of beatings, being unwanted, rampant discrimination" - "that these feelings of inadequacy in your life experience will never disappear completely." And in that moment something transformed. His perhaps paradoxical intervention worked. With as well some twenty years of work with the Erhard Seminar Training {EST] attending at least twenty-five seminars and several of their advanced programs, some lasting one year with a two times a week commitment lifted this blight of inadequacy, insufficiency and something is wrong here. That is to say while the past is the past, what I was able to do was "to put the past in the past and to keep it there".

I had previously had two other mentoring relationships; one for approximately seven years and another for about ten years that ran concurrently, I had a co-worker, Andrew during 1964 through 1972 where I was the Credit & Collection Manager. We would meet at least once a week for lunch while we were in the company and after some employment transitions. Discernment involved a central question or issue and then expanding my awareness of central themes, beliefs, patterns and most importantly strategies to breakthrough to more effective outcomes. One such discovery was a perpetual pattern of being late and with ample justifications and rationalizations. I remember distinctly that in one of those lunches he said my lateness was a blatant disrespect to him and he said that one more lateness would result in ending our weekly meetings. He appeared resolute and highly challenged by consistent pattern. We sat in silence for some period of time when the meaning of his words became a reality. I had never looked at lateness as disrespect.

Respect is the cornerstone of the Bushido Code of Behavior and he had discerned the very essence of what would cause a shift in my behavior; I was never ever late again and needed to make that declaration before I left. Perhaps this is a small accomplishment, however, the how and when to construct my day had to reestablish priorities, to give my word with integrity on assignments as being late had wider implications than being late for an appointment, it was also being late for my family and a myriad of other life issues. Ultimately, from this realization my acceptance of respect filled many other corridors of living life competently with joy and satisfaction. Those who share their greatness and empowerment skills give us access to our unexpressed genius. Those who prove the world is not flat take with them on their voyage a belief system that eventually touches a new world reality. It is important to be a generating force of life, to inspire, contribute, and cause people to un-conceal their unexpressed greatness. In making such contributions to others, people grow as flowers, blooming in the orchard of mankind. When we leave this planet, we can only hope that we have harvested plains and valleys and mountain peaks of realized beings by contributing to their greatness.

The next ten years my formal mentorship was transferred by Andrew to Lee, the Wizard, beginning about 1981 when I ended my career in the financial world as a Manager of Financial Services. There were so many realizations and positive accomplishment, but the pinnacle realization was when he asked me, "Do you know whose voice that is?" It was the first time I had identified a voice as giving me insight and understanding about the workings of my world and possible outcomes yet to come outside myself.

The voice always seemed to be part of my internal dialogue; and, therefore, I never thought of the voice as being any other than my own, perhaps just at a different frequency. I did identify mystical properties and a natural knowingness about the voice. Perhaps that voice, in attempting to name it over a life-time, could belong to Joshua. I am not absolutely sure. It was never really essential to name the voice.

The Promesa Emergence of Acceptance and Going On

I will never forget one Saturday, my first visit to the Executive Director's home. He was surrounded by at least four or five major political figures, friends of absolute commitment to PROMESA and its legacy to the Hispanic community.

As I walked up the driveway I could identify the entourage of prominent people. Obviously not being Puerto Rican the group grew silent. I realized I was completely out of my element and perhaps in some way intruding. Executive Director said in Spanish, "This is my very good friend George." The way he said it in Spanish meant he personally sanctioned my presence. I was to be trusted and most importantly their conversation could continue in the same vein. I was thunderstruck. Such an acknowledgment to a non-Puerto Rican was absolutely astounding. I realized at that moment the trust and confidence that Executive Director had in me; in effect he had said, "This man is one of us; I personally vouch for him." God oftentimes finds moments to reward his servants and in this one moment I was soaring: a prominent

Puerto Rican New York political power collective was accepting me. To be accepted by anyone, especially this body of men was to know I was known as "count-on-able" "reliable" "trustworthy".

It happened again at the annual Gala, held once each year in September at the Marriott Hotel on Broadway and 45 Street. There I sat with Executive Director and his wife, and other congressional personages. So many others more worthy than me were not given this notable acknowledgement and confirmation.

God gives each and every one of us moments in time to realize that if we keep our commitment to excellence and work toward the betterment of mankind, we may sit at the table of wisdom and power and to be recognized as contribution. Thank you, God, for your bountiful gifts that complement the past, that give us sanction and acceptance in the present, and most importantly that allow us to be seen as someone who makes a difference, for that is the greatest contribution I can demonstrate while I serve others.

One evening while I was at PROMESA, I received a call from a doctor, a call which I initially missed because I was in the gym. My mother was in a Bronx nursing home at the time, and I thought the call was about her. Once the person on phone duty that night located me, he said he would notify me when the doctor called again; the doctor had indicated that the matter was important and he would call me back shortly.

I got the high sign about ten minutes later and answered the call. He said, "I have your résumé here, and I am very interested." I asked him the name of his company and he said, "MTA New York City Transit." Within a flashing reflective moment I said, "I don't believe that I sent you a résumé." I thought perhaps this was the

Executive Office testing me to see if I was interested in another job opportunity since I had sent no resume. Then he asked, "Do you know who this is?" I knew that voice; it was Rick who had been on my staff and who had subsequently left our employ. I wondered aloud, "Considering the circumstances in which you left, why would you want to hire me?" He said, "I will never forget our relationship or how you treated me. I would like you to interview for this job opportunity." We arranged a time for the coming week in Brooklyn.

I quickly called home and asked my wife if she knew anything about mailing a résumé to Transit and she said she did. She said we had discussed it and I said, "Absolutely not."

My questioning was intense and accusatory. I began to argue with my wife about why she had sent a résumé and probably a cover letter which I had not seen or signed. The conversation was short-lived when she said, "Are you arguing with me that you have a job interview? Seems as if he's interested in hiring you, no?"

I had worked with Transit's Employee Assistance Program [EAP] for the past twelve years, since June 1993. I moved from being on call at PROMESA, with twelve hour work days, serving on almost all their committees, being an integral part of community outreach and advocacy work to a position at Transit which is 8:00 A.M. to 4:00 P.M., Monday through Friday. Ultimately, when I reviewed Sunday's The New York Times job posting, the position read "Ph.D. required." The job needed to be down-graded so they could hire me, and I subsequently pursued my Ph.D.

Once again, "I thank you, God, for your extraordinary interventions, contributions and the serendipity of your miraculous work in my life."

Locating a Lawyer to Close on the Space of Miracles

I had located the property in Margaretville, New York, and required a lawyer. I was told by the voice to find a place for the Space of Miracles and God would provide me with the money and I would do the work. At the time we were staying at a Bed and Breakfast called in Fleischmann, New York. The proprietor recommended that I use Diego Martin and said that while he was having his annual Christmas gathering, he was in one of the two rooms and asked if I remembered him. I said I had not met him, took the number and called him from home the following week. I introduced myself and then I heard the voice. My first question was, "Were you in the building on the corner street before you drive up the road just past the street light in Margaretville?" He responded that he had been. I then asked him, "Do you have an interest in buying that building?" He said he had been there that very morning and made an offer to buy or rent the building. Several minutes later I asked if I might ask him a question about his physical health and he gave me a clear go ahead. I was sitting down at my rolltop desk and asked for a minute, as I took a metal ruler and measured off certain dimensions and asked him so many inches in that direction and so many inches in that direction "Are you experiencing some pressure?" He asked, "Do you think it's my lungs or my heart?" I said, "It feels like a muscle spasm of some kind." He said, "I need to go to New York to see a specialist and I have been postponing it." Interesting that at no time did Diego ask how I knew what I knew?

Rev. EK: The Television Seminary Video

———— ❦ ————

I had some scope of responsibility in arranging the annual EAP Grand Rounds at my job at that time. I had attended one of the monthly meetings at the Employee Assistance Professional Association [EAPA], customarily held the third Tuesday of each month at one of the various hospitals, institutes, academic institutions such as treatment programs in the New York City area. At the meeting, Carla, a colleague, showed an excellent video on prejudicial behavior and working through these issues in a group setting. After a brief telephone conversation she invited me and my wife to her home in Conn. She was cordial, worldly, and well-read – and her house was clearly a spiritual center. I was surprised to learn she was an ordained minister, having graduated from the oldest interfaith seminary in the United States. On Sunday My wife and I attended a service in her home, her customary Sunday service. As part of the service we read round robin from a leading text, beginning where the group had left off from the prior Sunday. Some of the eight participants shared their experiences from the previous week, a happening which gave each person an opportunity to partially integrate the teachings from the reading and contribute from their lives.

The service included a prayer circle for those needing help with health or with other aspects of their lives. Carla prayed for the health and wellbeing of those family members and friends who had some life affliction. As the group began to socialize after the service was completed, two of the women shared their experiences with me about the formation of the and interfaith seminary which had just begun its first year. Their joint learning experiences were very engaging and their religious fervor was spiritually inspiring. At that moment the face of one of the two women turned into a miniature television and the next thing I knew, I was in the classroom with the thirty or so students, observing the class in progress. I became aware that I was transfixed and having an out of body experience and shared that experience with the two students after my brief video escapade, as I call the interlude – this was in my interpretation God's divine intervention that altered and transported my state of consciousness. Immediate outreach was made to the Dean of the School, and it appeared as if I would be considered as a divinity student. I needed to forward my credentials and life experience to the dean's home. She indicated that my credentials appeared adequate for immediate consideration. Their origin was a church which broke away from its traditional affiliation during the Vietnam conflict and formed the Interfaith Community Church. The following weekend I traveled to my first weekend learning experience, where my first classroom session was in Pennsylvania, was conducted in an annex adjacent to the church, exactly as I had envisioned it in my instant video replay --- the people, seating arrangement, book cases and classroom setup were exactly as I had envisioned them.

My experience from the end of 2000 through December 2002, when I was ordained an Interfaith Minister, led to a deepening of my faith, an awakening of the importance of God in my life, and the realization that the Interfaith Church enabled me to reach out to all peoples everywhere and not to be isolated or entrenched in one belief, one dogma, one way of understanding my relationship with God. Thank you once again God, for creating an entry way to serve you and to learn more about the many religions and beliefs that create our world and interactions with one another.

To be in the right place at the right time with extraordinary insight, understanding and guidance represents God's divine plan. Through the many gifts of the spirit, may my contributions be generative and contributory, inspire wisdom and love and be directed toward making a difference in the lives of all peoples everywhere.

The Magnificent Readings in Montreal Canada

During an annual international conference in May of 2002, I intended to do twelve readings in the same area that other readers were doing theirs, but I would do mine for free. Joan Loys, Ph.D., did a Lakota rock reading for me, and my question to her concerned the appropriateness of doing God's work at my Space of Miracles location in Margaretville, N.Y. Her reading indicated that I should proceed.

During the next annual conference in May of 2003 I chose not to do any readings, but to use that time for myself to absorb the many sessions throughout the day. However, close to the last day my close friend, Gary, asked me to do a healing. I cleared myself, performed a preliminary body reading, closed my eyes and began the engagement process. What I visualized in an eyes-closed healing process was that parts of the left side of his body were missing. I then began the restoration process to reconstruct those areas. When I came out of my trance state, he reported that my observations were accurate and he was being treated for some neurological conditions. When I finished the healing, he said that he was able to stand on his left foot which was his presenting complaint and felt restored.

Later that day he asked if I would work with his wife and I said I would. She was already sitting quietly apart. Marina is quiet, reserved, deeply compassionate and insightful. She and her sister are well known in the Indian community as inspired women and psychic healers.

I immediately sensed a presence in my work and the voice gave me very specific information. The information was extraordinarily penetrating and of concern, and I needed to ask if I could share the information and if I should proceed given the gravity of the information revealed. The information concerned the presence of a child that had not been birthed, but had a real and important presence in her life. I said that in order for her to be released from this image and presence, a healing might be helpful. In her true magnificence she allowed me to proceed and accepted my offering to enter her sacred selfdom. The healing was extensive, mostly my entering her realm of reality, aligning with her presence and at some point holding her hands, and joining the spirit of the unborn with the wanting and caring of her spirit. There were words spoken, ideas formulated and spiritual energies intermingled, and deep healing work absorbed. Upon exiting from this healing experience, we both sat quietly, reverently, filled with generous beginnings and letting go of old endings.

She told me, "Many, many years ago I met with one of our most powerful shamans. He told me that there was an unborn child, just as you did, and the other things you said were almost exactly what he told me." She reported that she felt comforted and made whole. The tears in her eyes disappeared and she asked to sit for a while to absorb the many blessings that were present. I felt energized and have made a contribution knew that in the presence of other healing channels and spiritually aligned spaces the doors of wisdom and contribution are always open.

Thank You God, A Daily Prayer

From my reading these experiences, it dawned on me that throughout the day I thank God multiple times. Sometimes that thankfulness arises when I perform some good interaction with a client, or when I eat, or I walk down a hallway or up a flight of stairs, and at other unimportant, seemingly insignificant times as well. Prayer to me occurs as a habit of acknowledgment throughout the day and this, in my understanding of my relationship with God, marks its specialness. 'Thank you, God' is not relegated to the getting times in life which are filled with abundance and having.

Giving thanks to God is many heart-felt moments throughout the day when I feel gratitude and obedience to a higher calling, living inside of His generosity and abundance.

Thank You, God, is a calling that occurs throughout the day just because one feels the flow and glow of His blessings. Abundance is always there as are forgiveness and love; His presence is always there and accessible.

I believe that I live inside of His eternal flame and my voice sparks a light of identification and relatedness as I say 'Thank You, God.'

When I say these three simple words, I tend to repeat the phrase multiple times in quick succession and during those moments, what is released inside me is a sense of His contribution and His all pervading love. God is Good and God is Great.

Results and Beginnings

One's life is a collage of collective experiences building momentum toward multiple expressions of creativity and contribution.

The culmination of all these experiences created the direction of my life: to make a contribution, to support breakthrough experiences, to cause extraordinary outcomes in people's lives. I believe in our ability to generate miracles in our lives.

The miraculous voice and divine guidance led me to Margaretville, New York, where I located a mountain top paradise, which has been blessed by Micmac elders Albert and Archie Checho, and faces south overlooking the Papacton Reservoir and sequential mountain ranges.

A family of eagles nest somewhere on the mountain peaks and circles over head in the noon day sun. In a cave beneath the cliff I experienced a brilliant light, ten times ten more powerful than any glowing light I have ever seen, a light which glistened and spun sunbeams.

There was no apparent break in the surface of the cliff to account for this brilliant lightning.

This is the atmosphere which supports The Space of Miracles, a one-day journey, an experiential workshop, a catalyst, creating an environment for transforming our reality and having a life filled with 'miraculous' results. This is the home of The Space of Miracles Center. It has been cradled in a lifetime experience that Samurais Don't Cry.

As living has taught me, life offers limitless opportunities to generate miracles. One just has to be available to them.

The Space of Miracles is an exploration of the nature of extraordinary occurrences where participants have an opportunity to experience how they are able to access their intentions. We investigate beliefs and practices of materializing 'unreasonable' goals. We talk about miracles from our own experiences.

My life is a miracle and God is Good and God is Great; they go hand in hand; one can never ever separate one from the other.

My goal in life is to continue to share the abundance that is everywhere and never ever limited by circumstances; stops, blocks, halting conditions are just places to readjust our focus to recalibrate and move toward the light of committed action. Stop signs are resting places to realign our relationship to God and to channel one day at a time to know our will shall be done through surrender.

Listen, listen, and listen to one's inner voice of natural knowing which emerges when there is non-attachment to an outcome, only a sense of building and standing in his presence on holy ground. We are standing on holy ground, and I know there are angles all round. Let us praise God now, praise him, we are standing in his sweet presence on holy ground.

Printed in the United States
by Baker & Taylor Publisher Services